RENDEZVOUS WITH RETIREMENT:
A Guide to Getting Fiscally Fit

James C. Molet

RENDEZVOUS WITH RETIREMENT: A Guide to Getting Fiscally Fit

Published by JCM Publishing, Sierra Vista, AZ 85635.

ISBN: 978-0-9895505-7-4

RENDEZVOUS WITH RETIREMENT: A Guide to Getting Fiscally Fit

Book cover image provided courtesy of Dallas Smith.
For permission to use material within this book please contact James C. Molet:
jcm.publishing@yahoo.com

Subscribe to the http://RetirementSavvy.net blog, where personal finance, with a focus on retirement planning, is covered via Discussions, Recommendations, Interviews, Quizzes and the Living Frugally series. This book contains information obtained from authentic and highly regarded sources. Reprinted material is quoted with permission and sources are cited.

CONTENTS

ACKNOWLEDGMENTS

Sincere gratitude and thanks are extended to the following who helped to bring this Second Edition into being:

My wife, Karen, the partner that makes most of my successes possible.

Mr. Brian Tramuel, a long-time reader of my blog, for his continued support of the blog and his kind, thoughtful words in the Foreword.

All those that have shared their wisdom with me over the years. This book is dedicated to the idea that knowledge should be shared, particularly knowledge that has the ability to profoundly change lives. If only a handful of people are able to benefit from this book and improve their financial well-being, the effort in writing it has been well worth it.

INTRODUCTION

I retired in 2005 after serving 21 years in the United States Army, where I had a chance to travel the world and engage with a diverse, eclectic group of people and enjoy incredible experiences. During the latter part of my career, my interest in personal finance was piqued based on my own experiences and observations of the way most Americans plan – or more accurately, fail to plan – for retirement and the difficulty many face in starting the process. During this period I made a concentrated effort to understand key personal finance terminology, concepts and philosophies.

During the course of my journey to achieving fiscal fitness, I have often spoken to family and friends about the topics of budgeting, saving, investing, and preparing for retirement. However, it seems as though I often feel like I forgot a key point or did not give better context to something that I may have mentioned.

This book serves multiple purposes. It allows me to reflect on my own journey to become fiscally fit and achieve financial freedom; it serves as a practical guide for those looking for a way to establish a financial foundation and prepare for retirement; and it serves as a way to give family and friends a means of verifying the things we may have discussed, capturing some of the finer points which I may have missed during the course of our conversations. I am hopeful that those who may be struggling with personal finances find value in its pages.

James C. Molet

PREFACE

Broke. Touching down in Denver on a flight from Korea in 1994, that reality struck me like a lightning bolt. Arriving at Fort Bragg, North Carolina a few weeks later - following a short visit with my family in Denver - the first observable instance of my new financial situation presented itself as I had just enough money for the first month's rent and security deposit on a small apartment. My wife and I had separated during the year that I was in Korea and I was placed in a difficult position financially. Not only had she failed to make our car payments for a few months, but she had also sold all of our belongings during the time that I was gone. Fortunately, my parents were able to help me get the car payments caught up, ensuring I would have a means of transportation while at Fort Bragg.

To make the situation even more bleak, it would be a few weeks before the few belongings I did have would arrive from Korea. As I did not have the money for bedding, again I was fortunate to have supportive parents, as they had given me some blankets and pillows during my visit to Denver. Without a radio, a television (I could not afford cable TV anyway), furniture, or the money to do anything, I found myself bedding down on the living room floor (it was cooler than the bedroom) and going to sleep once the sun set during those first few weeks in my new apartment. Broke.

It was during that period I adopted the pizza (Mr. P's frozen pizza, $0.69 each if memory serves me correctly), chicken ramen, and orange juice diet. Not a great diet from a nutritional perspective, but definitely inexpensive! There were probably 100 different aspects of struggling financially during that period that I would sometimes recall, and occasionally still do. However, the pizza, ramen, and orange juice diet; along with rationing money and giving plasma for cash are the most vivid.

I distinctly remember pumping $1.50 worth of gas at a time because I was typically down to my last $8 or so and I did not want to spend it all on gas lest something come up before the next pay day. While I was not able to get a second job at that time, I was able to give plasma. Got plasma? You bet! Prior to arriving at Fort Bragg, I had never heard of giving plasma for money. However, in speaking with a co-worker about my difficulties in making ends meet, he alerted me to the practice. While it was not much, $10 during the first visit and another $20 if you came back within two weeks, it was a much needed extra $30/month for someone putting only $1.50 worth of gas at a time in the tank. I have no idea how many times I paid $1.50 - $3.00 for gas or gave plasma; however, it had to be the better part of a year as it took me that long to get on my feet again, or at least what passed for on my feet at that time.

Flash forward to 2001. A prolonged separation and attempted reconciliation ended where it should have seven years previously, with a divorce. At this point I was thirty-four years old, active duty in the United States Army for 17 years - half of my life - and living like many Americans, paycheck to paycheck. My financial situation had not improved over the years and now a divorce. Soon after my divorce was finalized during the spring of that year, I sat down one afternoon to assess where I was financially. Initially my focus was on the near-term, just trying to keep my head above water for the moment and evaluating how I was positioned on a monthly basis. It was not promising as my monthly expenses slightly exceeded my monthly income. Broke.

While I went to work right away at reducing my expenses, there was a brief period, perhaps three to four months, before I finally deeply considered the long-term implications of living paycheck to paycheck, some months running a slight deficit, others a slight surplus. Although I do not recall the exact date or moment that my life changed significantly, it was during that period. Conducting the assessment of where I was at that point in 2001 and reflecting on my financial struggles a few years previously lit a fire within me. Soon thereafter I committed myself to changing my fiscal well-being.

Although I had managed to save a little bit of money at various times earlier in my life, I was never able to sustain any real savings momentum; always derailed by an emergency here or an unexpected expense there. At one time, in the early 1990s, I had invested in my first mutual fund before I really had an idea how they worked and before I had a long-term savings and investment plan. While I intuitively understood that I should be doing something, the specifics escaped me. Unfortunately, I did not maintain the mutual fund as some emergency or another prompted me to close the account - paying a penalty in the process of course - and take the cash.

Just as I had always prided myself on being physically fit, it was during this period in my life that I firmly committed to the idea of being fiscally fit as well. Just as being physically fit involves two components, controlling diet and exercising; being fiscally fit also involves two components, controlling debt and investing. Fourteen years later, lots of self-taught education, a new marriage, and an investment portfolio performing better than expected, my second wife, whom I married in 2008, and I are fiscally fit and excited about preparing for retirement.

You should understand what this book is and what it is not. This book serves as a personal reflection on my journey as well as a guide for those that might find themselves in a situation similar to mine in 2001 and are looking to right their financial ship and prepare for retirement. If you are sick and tired of being sick and tired, this book is for you. It provides guidelines for how to determine how much money you will need - or desire - in retirement, actions associated with retirement planning, behaviors you should adopt to become fiscally fit, provides tools to assist you and highlights various philosophies. Additionally, it provides some guidelines for funding your chosen retirement accounts. In short, its aim is to help you become a consumer of personal finance information and become more savvy as you work toward retirement.

This book is not an attempt to sell any product or service, nor does it suggest that there is an easy path to acquiring wealth and preparing for a comfortable retirement. There is no magic bullet. While you will find recommendations for fund types, you will not find any recommendations for specific stocks or mutual funds, as you will have to perform detailed research on your own to determine which underlying investments will make up your retirement accounts. Just like achieving and maintaining physical health requires a detailed plan, committed effort, and focus, so does achieving and maintaining fiscal health.

I do not possess any formal finance related credentials, nor do I seek any. A lot of what I learned was self-taught by reading every finance related publication I could find over the course of a two to three-year period, visiting numerous finance and retirement related web sites, a few formal courses during the pursuit of my undergraduate degree and MBA, and lots of conversations with some smart, savvy friends. The motivation to continue learning more comes from my own observations of how – or perhaps more accurately, people do not – manage their money and prepare for retirement. This phenomenon is captured in studies conducted by the Employee Benefit Research Institute® (EBRI) and reports issued by the Bureau of Labor Statistics (BLS), two great sources of information.

FOREWORD

The catalyst for most to change is to find bottom. Bottom is where we separate fantasy from reality, consciously assessing our options against possible solutions. Imagine yourself in financial bondage; the demand for instant gratification, irresponsible spending, preoccupation with what's new and abuse of credit cards. It wasn't until I lost the ability to maintain this "I owe, I owe, so off to work I go" lifestyle that I realized my bottom and decided to take decisive action. With my income drastically reduced I had to think different; what if my income represented an opportunity for the future instead of an obligation to the past? How we spend our money tells a story; how much could you save and invest? How much could you give? How much could you blow and just have fun with? This internal head versus heart battle is the inspiration behind James Molet's guide to getting fiscally fit. If your financial story has friction, spark a fire so that you are able to achieve the story your heart desires.

Rendezvous With Retirement is a practical guide for the one thing the average family is missing in their financial story; a plan. Why do you want to change your story? What will it look like when you're done? Follow along as James provides a real world approach; a blueprint to finding your balance and courage in living for today and preparing for tomorrow.

By the time I finished reading Rendezvous With Retirement I had adapted several new ways to thinking different. How we define wealth, "You are wealthy when you and your family can live your chosen lifestyle on portfolio and passive income; and no longer require earned income" and how we relate physical fitness to fiscal fitness, "Just as being physically fit involves two components, controlling diet and exercising; being fiscally fit also involves two components, controlling debt and investing." Those are two of my favorites, however there are many more quotables for better thinking.

I follow James C. Molet on his blog retirement savvy dot net where it serves as an extension to this book, living better through planning. I applaud James as he continues to share his knowledge, even providing personal information to show why his voice is relevant to the conversation. The context here within as well as the content on his blog communicates as strongly as content.

Brian D. Tramuel

[1] HONESTLY ASSESS YOUR SITUATION AND ADJUST

As many people are aware, divorce often has significant financial implications for both parties. Not unlike a lot of people before me, I found myself in serious financial straits following my divorce in 2001. Not only did I not have adequate savings to fall back on, an emergency fund, but a quick review of my finances after the divorce was finalized revealed that my monthly financial expenses typically exceeded my monthly income by a few dollars. In short, at thirty-four years of age and on active duty in the United States Army for 17 years, I was essentially broke.

How could I have stuck with one organization in one career and not have done a better job of managing my finances I wondered? It was not as if I was changing jobs every few years scrambling to make a few dollars more an hour or secure better benefits. Soon thereafter I committed myself to changing my fiscal well-being. Just as I had always prided myself on being physically fit, it was then that I decided it was just as important to be fiscally fit.

My first order of business was to conduct a detailed analysis of my financial obligations such as credit cards, car loan, child support, rent, food, utilities; and develop a spending plan. Second, I researched ways in which I could eliminate or lower (e.g. change cable TV from an upper tier service to the basic service) the cost of each of those obligations on a monthly basis. Fortunately, during this period of my Army career I was traveling quite a bit in support of Operations Iraqi Freedom and Enduring Freedom which provided extra pay associated with duties in those areas.

That travel provided the added bonus of helping reduce some monthly expenses such as utilities and gas simply because, for long periods of time, I was able to avoid a lot of the expenses (e.g. gas, electricity, water, etc.) associated with driving to work on a daily basis and maintaining a residence. As I began to travel less – and my income was reduced – I picked up a second, part-time job, working a few hours each night on weekday evenings and eight hour shifts on weekends at a regional retail store. Generating extra income provides tremendous benefits; granted, not a lot of sleep at times, but extra income.

The combination of reducing numerous monthly expenses and eliminating some; and earning additional income, while on temporary duty in combat areas and picking up a second job, turned what was normally a slight monthly deficit into a monthly surplus which allowed me to develop a spending plan with savings and investments, vice debt, as the focal point. Once you have suffered under the burden of debt for awhile, the freedom financial control brings is liberating.

Surveying the Retirement Landscape

While some American families are fiscally fit and confidently executing their plan for retirement, unfortunately that is not the case for far too many Americans. A cursory glance of newspaper headlines or surfing news sites on the Internet on any day of the week communicates that very clearly. After reading numerous news stories and conversations with family and friends, my experience has been that most families generally fall into one of four groups. The first group simply has no understanding, and no real desire, to learn more regarding saving and investing for their future. Often their focus in on living solely for the moment, certain that things will somehow work out in the future. Winning a lottery perhaps? Or maybe hitting it big in Las Vegas? The second group understands that they should be doing something, but are not sure where to start. That is exactly where I was in the early 2000s.

The third group is saving and investing something; however, they are doing it blindly and could not tell you why they chose their particular investment products, have no discernible way to tell if they are saving enough for retirement and they do not know how much they will need to sustain them in retirement. The fourth group has at least the broad outlines of a plan in place, has used some type of calculator to quantify how much they should be saving and is actively engaged in managing their finances with an eye on the future. While I am hopeful that as many people as possible, from each of the four groups will read this book, the focus is really on the second and third groups. The 2014 Retirement Confidence Survey® (RCS) from the Employee Benefit Research Institute (EBRI) highlights the Americans that make up these groups.

The survey illustrates numerous shortcomings with regards to the way in which Americans are preparing for retirement. The RCS notes that nearly two-thirds of workers (64%) report that they and/or their spouse have saved money for retirement. That is the good news. Unfortunately, that number is down from the 75% observed in 2009. The percentage of workers that say they are saving for retirement currently stands at 57%, a slight decline from the 58% in 2012, which continues the decline from the level of 65%, reported in 2009.

What should be alarming to anyone paying attention, 60% of workers report they and/or their spouse have less than $25,000 in total savings and investments (excluding their home and defined benefit plans). Even more unbelievably, that number includes 36% who have less than $1,000, which is up from the 28% observed in the 2013 RCS. Perhaps not surprisingly, the large majority of workers who have not saved for retirement indicate their assets total less than $1,000. Access to a workplace retirement plan is a significant factor with respect to total savings and investment. Over 90% of workers that do not have access to a workplace retirement plan reported having less than $25,000 in savings and investments. You read that right, 90%. Conversely, that number drops to 38% for those that have access to a workplace retirement plan.

Not surprisingly, workers who have done a retirement needs calculation tend to be considerably more confident about their ability to save the amount needed for retirement than those who have not done the calculation, despite the fact that those doing a calculation tend to cite higher retirement savings goals. Twenty-five percent who have done a calculation, compared with the 13% who have not, say they are very confident that they will be able to accumulate the amount they need. At the other end of the spectrum, 32% who have not done a calculation, compared with 14% who have, report they are not at all confident in their ability to save the needed amount (EBRI, 2014).

The result of those sobering numbers is that today, many workers are planning to work longer and delay retirement. Of course, if you are able to work longer, that will reduce the amount of money that is needed in retirement. The Congressional Budget Office (2004) estimates that for a median worker, delaying retirement from age 62 to 66, reduces the level of assets needed in retirement by about 42%. Delaying retirement again to age 70 reduces the assets needed in retirement by another 61%.

Interestingly, numerous recent studies have shown that a majority of workers are planning to work past the age of 65, many are planning to work past age 70, and some have no plans to ever retire. I know that *"working after you retire"* sounds oxymoronic, but unfortunately, that is what retirement is coming to mean for a large segment of our society. Finding a part-time job after a career is finished just to make ends meet. No thank you!

The problem with that plan, and I use the word *plan* loosely, is that many of these workers may not have a choice but to leave the work force due to illness or injury; or it may simply be the case that the physical demands associated with their particular job may prevent them from staying as long as they would like to or need to. Additionally, if they are laid off from one job, they may find it is very difficult to get back into the work force. A 2011 study conducted by the Heldrich Center for Workforce Development at Rutgers University (Van Horn & Zukin, 2011) found that 35% workers over the age of 50 said they are not going to be able to work as long as they had expected.

Other numbers from the study are equally sobering. Less than one in four workers (23%) over 50 years of age is working full time. Far more are unemployed and looking for work (35%) or are working part-time while searching for full-time work (6%). A little over one in five have left the labor market altogether. Even for those who found another job, reemployment came with significant sacrifices. Nearly half (48%) did not find a job for over a year, and when they did, it was likely in a different field and accompanied by a pay cut. Talk about pouring salt in the wound. Ouch! By a margin of 50% to 18%, more described their new jobs as a step down, not a step up.

A staggering number of those unemployed over age 50 have been struggling for a significant period of time. Eighty percent have been looking for over one year, including almost 50% who have been looking for more than two years. More are pessimistic than optimistic by a margin of two to one about finding a job in the near future, and some 63% of those over 50 believe they will never have another full-time job in their field. If that sounds depressing to you, it does to me also. Just under half (46%) expect to file for Social Security earlier than they wanted to; another 18% already have done so. One-third of those over 50 have no health insurance and half said they have already cut back on health care expenses. Do you still believe that simply planning to work longer, instead of committing to getting savvy and fiscally fit now, is a viable plan?

Analyze Monthly Expenses

Detailed analysis of your monthly expenses is the first step in developing a sound spending plan. Before you can determine how much money you can commit to savings and investments, and put to work for yourself, you must determine how your earned income is currently being disbursed. While some expenses (e.g. insurance and taxes) are fixed, many are variable. These are the expenses you want to analyze extensively as they offer the best chance for spending less and saving more. There are two critical elements to analyzing those expenses: ensuring you identify all obligations and being completely honest with yourself about the extent of those obligations.

Regarding identifying all obligations, most of us are paid on a bi-weekly basis and monthly is the time period that most people associate with making bill payments as that is when most come due. However, some payments are made at different intervals. An example of this is car insurance. I pay mine on a bi-annual basis. Other examples include payments such as dental or medical co-payments which are often made at irregular intervals, depending on when or how often those services are required. When analyzing expenses, make sure all are noted. Do not dismiss a debt because it is comparatively less than some of your other obligations or is not necessarily paid on a regular basis. You must note *all* expenses.

With regards to being honest about the extent of all financial obligations, people tend to think in general, instead of specific, terms. As an example, if you ask someone what they spend on gas each month, they are likely to note that they *probably* spend *x* number of dollars. Similarly, if someone is asked how much they owe on a credit card, it is unlikely that they will know the specific balance, the exact monthly payment, or the interest rate they are paying.

Utilizing a spreadsheet is an effective way to capture specific information regarding your expenses. I have created a spreadsheet, the RWR Spending Planner, which will help you with identifying and tracking your income and expenses. Additionally, I have developed the RWR Retirement Planner - covered in greater detail in **Chapter 5** - that captures all of the information required to develop your nest-egg number, makes it easy to track progress, make adjustments, and view all relevant retirement numbers on one easily read and understood document. Together they comprise the RWR Simple Retirement Workbook, available for download at the RetirementSavvy website [http://wp.me/p3JVpt-Wd] at no cost.

As some payments (e.g. electricity bill) will fluctuate a little month to month you will want to capture payment information over at least a three month period, ensuring that non-monthly payments are included in your calculations to accurately determine your average monthly financial output. Additionally, irregular payments such as those discussed previously must be accounted for. One potential option is to analyze payments made in recent years to develop a reasonable monthly average. Another consideration, if you are capturing this data during one particular time of the year (e.g. spring) and you know that certain bills (e.g. electricity) are much higher during different times of the year (e.g. winter); you might want to refer to previous bills or your account history to help determine an accurate average.

On the next two pages is the Smith Family Spending Plan (**Figure 1**) and (**Figure 2**), the fictional family we will use as an example throughout the book as we assess their fiscal fitness. As you can see, the Smith Family Spending Plan is comprised of typical monthly household expenses, broken down into groups such as Home, Daily Living, Transportation, Entertainment, Health, Personal and Financial Obligations.

Note that their average income over the three month period for the Smith clan is $3,887.07 ($11,661.20/3) while their average expenses are $3,983.20 ($11,949.61/3), leaving them with a monthly average deficit of $96.14 ($288.41/3). Other key takeaways from the Smith Family Spending Plan are that they currently are not contributing anything to their long-term savings or retirement accounts. Unfortunately, the Smith Family Spending Plan probably looks very similar to that of many American households, maybe even yours.

Smith Family Spending Plan				
	January	February	March	Total
INCOME				
Wages	3,875.25	3,900.50	3,885.45	11,661.20
Income totals	3,875.25	3,900.50	3,885.45	11,661.20
EXPENSES				
Home				
Mortgage/rent	1,585.00	1,585.00	1,585.00	4,755.00
Utilities	185.56	192.35	189.95	567.86
Telephone services	123.42	124.00	135.00	382.42
Home repairs	95.23	0.00	76.52	171.75
Internet service	45.00	45.00	45.00	135.00
Home improvement	125.00	56.00	95.52	276.52
Home totals	2,159.21	2,002.35	2,126.99	6,288.55
Daily living				
Groceries	352.00	328.95	276.90	957.85
Dry cleaning	42.00	56.50	50.00	148.50
Dining out	135.56	125.25	86.35	347.16
Daily living totals	529.56	510.70	413.25	1,453.51
Transportation				
Gas/fuel	85.00	89.54	76.24	250.78
Insurance	48.50	48.50	48.50	145.50
Repairs	25.56	0.00	63.24	88.80
Public transportation	0.00	0.00	0.00	0.00
Transportation totals	159.06	138.04	187.98	485.08

Figure 1. Smith Family Spending Plan

Smith Family Spending Plan, Continued				
	January	February	March	Total
Entertainment				
Cable TV	158.00	158.00	158.00	474.00
Video/DVD rentals	24.50	37.00	30.27	91.77
Movies/plays	46.00	52.25	75.50	173.75
Entertainment totals	228.50	247.25	263.77	739.52
Health				
Health club dues	75.00	75.00	75.00	225.00
Insurance	85.00	85.00	85.00	255.00
Prescriptions	25.50	35.00	35.00	95.50
Over-the-counter drugs	24.26	40.16	15.62	80.04
Health totals	209.76	235.16	210.62	655.54
Personal				
Clothing	58.52	62.45	82.09	203.06
Salon/barber	35.00	45.00	40.00	120.00
Books	15.25	0.00	20.45	35.70
Music (CDs, etc.)	30.25	25.65	45.25	101.15
Personal totals	139.02	133.10	187.79	459.91
Financial obligations				
Long-term savings	0.00	0.00	0.00	0.00
Retirement (401k, Roth IRA)	0.00	0.00	0.00	0.00
Credit card payments	452.00	505.50	650.00	1,607.50
Other obligations	85.00	150.00	25.00	260.00
Financial obligation totals	537.00	655.50	675.00	1,867.50
Total expenses	3,962.11	3,803.60	3,927.40	11,949.61
Cash short/extra	(86.86)	96.90	(41.95)	(288.41)

Figure 2. Smith Family Spending Plan, Continued

Reduce Monthly Expenses

The result of tracking your monthly expenses over a given time period will obviously yield one of two results. Either your monthly income will exceed your monthly financial obligations or vice versa. More importantly however, it will give you a clear view of how you are currently allocating your money. As we have observed, the Smiths are currently hovering right around the breakeven point each month with an average monthly deficit of $96.14. In either case, particularly if your monthly expenses exceed your monthly income, like the Smiths, you want to find every way possible to reduce your monthly expenses. Additionally, you should explore ways to increase your income, with finding a second job the most obvious solution. Working a second job is not easy, but there may be times when it is necessary. Believe me, I speak from experience. During the latter half of my Army career, there were two periods (totaling about two years) when I picked up second jobs to increase income. Attacking the problem on two fronts (similar to improving diet and exercising with regards to physical fitness) is the ideal approach.

There are literally hundreds of ways to reduce your monthly expenses. I suggest starting with the two categories of expenses that have the most significant impact on most households: housing and transportation. The 2012 Consumer Expenditure Survey notes that housing accounts for 33% of expenditures annually while transportation accounts for 17% (Bureau of Labor Statistics, 2014). Analyzing those two items first, listed are some reduction options with regards to housing: move into a smaller house (or an apartment), refinance your home mortgage, terminate services such as lawn care or housecleaning, cancel or reduce cable TV service, start purchasing generic cleaning supplies and adjust cooling/heating up or down a couple degrees as appropriate depending on the time of year. With regards to transportation: sell one car if you currently have two or more, join a carpool or vanpool, ride a bike to work (which nicely supports both fiscal and physical fitness objectives), or start utilizing public transportation.

Debt. Described as the amount of money that you owe to a person, a bank, a company, etc. or the state of owing money to someone or something. When we hear that word – debt – most of us think of the first definition and cringe. It is an uncomfortable feeling knowing that we owe a given sum of money to a person, a bank, or a company. Unfortunately, very few of us are able to get through life without debt touching our lives, particularly as younger adults, when it is nearly impossible not to accrue some debt in pursuit of higher education, an automobile or a home.

A significant expense for many American households is credit card debt, which is staggering. The average credit card debt per American household is

$15,799, the percent of disposable income paid to service credit card debt is 13.9%, the percentage of cardholders whose balance is over $10,000 is 15%, the percent who said their debt had increased in the past 12 months is 26%, and the average debt of a college graduate is $20,000 (Statistic Brain, 2012). I could go on and on, but my guess is that you get the picture. Debt, particularly credit card debt, is a scourge on our society and the greatest inhibitor to getting fiscally fit and successfully executing a solid retirement plan.

Every person that has dealt with debt, and I am guessing that is most of us, understands the tension, the anxiety that often comes with it. The mental oppression, that sinking feeling when the monthly payment comes due and there isn't enough money to make a payment…or make the payment in full. Worse yet, thinking about the number of years it will take to satisfy the debt! It should not come as a surprise that there is a psychological impact to carrying debt. Recently, a study by the Feinberg School of Medicine at Northwestern University concluded that there are physical impacts as well. Among the findings is that a higher debt-to-asset ratio is associated with higher perceived stress and depression, worse self-reported general health; and higher diastolic blood pressure. Additionally, individuals with greater debt were found to have a 1.3 percent increase (relative to the mean) in diastolic blood pressure.

What does that mean? Debt, which obviously negatively impacts your fiscal well-being, also negatively impacts your mental and physical well-being. On the flip side, the opposite must also be true. Ridding yourself of debt improves your fiscal, physical and mental well-being. Therefore, while it should go without saying, I will say it anyway, *"stop using your credit cards!"* One option for reducing existing credit card debt is to request an interest rate reduction from the card issuer.

When speaking with the customer service agent, ensure that you point out your excellent payment history, which hopefully that is the case, and the number of years you have been a loyal customer. A second option is to seek a credit card consolidation loan. As the name suggests, this type of loan consolidates multiple higher rate credit cards into one lower rate loan which translates to paying less overall interest while you are paying down the balance. Subsequently the loan will allow you to pay off the total amount sooner than you could pay off the same amount at a higher interest rate, freeing up money to commit to your savings and investment plan. Similar to requesting an interest rate reduction, the better and longer your relationship with your bank, the more likely you will receive an approval.

With regards to paying off credit card debt, one school of thought is that credit cards with higher interest rates should be paid off first while the other school of thought suggests paying off those with the lowest balances first is the way to go. From a purely financial perspective, the former is the better approach. However, there is value in the latter approach as there is a psychological lift – a real sense of progress – from paying off one card and then committing the money that was being paid on the first to the next card in line, continuing this progression until the last card is paid off. This was the approach I took and it worked well for me. Whichever method you use, the key is to stop using the credit cards and stay committed to reducing the balances to zero while you start working your savings and investment plan.

That last point brings us to another case of differing schools of thought. One philosophy suggests that credit card debt should be paid off completely prior to committing money to investing. My belief is that while credit card debt should be under control and be on a steady decline, it does not necessarily need to be paid off completely before you develop a savings and investment plan and begin committing money to your retirement accounts. The rationale is that the sooner you establish your savings and investment accounts, get in the habit of funding them, and get in the habit of managing them the better off you will be; the sooner you can make your money start working for you through the power of compound interest. The power of compound interest is covered later in **Chapter 3** and **Chapter 4**. If you would like to consider the question of paying off debt first vice paying off debt and investing at the same time, I encourage you research the question in greater detail. Numerous tools, such as Morningstar's® Solution Worksheet, are available online to help you explore the various implications of committing to one before the other or performing the actions in concert.

Additional options for reducing monthly expenses include eating out less, canceling magazine subscriptions, modifying telephone service, and reducing entertainment costs (e.g. renting/streaming videos vice going to a movie theater). These are only some of the ways in which you can reduce your expenses. You are only limited by your imagination and the level of commitment to ridding yourself of debt. When viewing your spreadsheet with all of your obligations, you should find some way, being as creative as necessary, to reduce most, if not each and every expense.

Increase Income

While the options for increasing income might not be as plentiful as the options for reducing monthly expenses, there are a number of ways in which it can be done. The first consideration should be to look no further than your current employer. Options there include asking for a raise, pursuing a promotion, volunteering for overtime, or volunteering for special assignments within your organization that offer proficiency/special duty pay. If no options exist within your present place of employment, consider outside options. If pride is an inhibitor, for your own good put it aside! There is absolutely no shame in picking up a second job at a supermarket, retailer, or restaurant for additional income. Would you rather pick up a job delivering pizzas or continue to suffer under the weight of your debt? Remember, the income from any part-time job will go a long way toward helping reduce your monthly expenses and increasing the money available for funding your retirement accounts.

Looking at the Updated Smith Family Spending Plan (**Figure 3**) and (**Figure 4**), we can see that they have taken some steps (highlighted in yellow) to increase their income and lower their expenses. For the Smiths, Robert found a weekend part-time job with a lawn service company earning $200/month, while Judy started to carpool with a co-worker that lives in her neighborhood, reducing the amount they spend on gas by 25%, cutting her half of their gas expense in half. Together they decided to better manage their use of gas and electricity, replace their premium Internet service (50 Mbps) with the basic package (12 Mbps), replace their premium cable service with the basic package, replace some nights out a movie theater or play with watching movies at home, cancel their health club memberships (doing more running/exercises at home), buy fewer new clothes, and reduce the purchase of new music by 50%. The final action the Smiths took was to get a loan - at a lower rate than the average of the cards - to consolidate their credit card debt, reducing their monthly payments to $400. Note that the Smith's new average income over a three month period is up to $4087.06 ($12,261.20/3) while their monthly average expenses are down to $3,570.29 ($10,710.87/3), flipping their average deficit of $96.13 to an average surplus of $516.78 ($1,550.33/3). Now the Smiths are turning their wayward ship around.

Smith Family Spending Plan				
	April	May	June	Total
INCOME				
Wages	4,075.25	4,100.50	4,085.45	12,261.20
Income totals	4,075.25	4,100.50	4,085.45	12,261.20
EXPENSES				
Home				
Mortgage/rent	1,585.00	1,585.00	1,585.00	4,755.00
Utilities	145.26	155.28	148.85	449.39
Telephone services	123.42	124.00	135.00	382.42
Home repairs	95.23	0.00	76.52	171.75
Internet service	30.00	30.00	30.00	90.00
Home improvement	125.00	56.00	95.52	276.52
Home totals	2,103.91	1,950.28	2,070.89	6,125.08
Daily living				
Groceries	352.00	328.95	276.90	957.85
Dry cleaning	42.00	56.50	50.00	148.50
Dining out	135.56	125.25	86.35	347.16
Daily living totals	529.56	510.70	413.25	1,453.51
Transportation				
Gas/fuel	63.75	67.16	57.18	188.09
Insurance	48.50	48.50	48.50	145.50
Repairs	25.56	0.00	63.24	88.80
Public transportation	0.00	0.00	0.00	0.00
Transportation totals	137.81	115.66	168.92	422.39

Figure 3. Updated Smith Family Spending Plan

Smith Family Spending Plan, Continued				
	April	May	June	Total
Entertainment				
Cable TV	95.00	95.00	95.00	285.00
Video/DVD rentals	30.00	40.25	30.50	100.75
Movies/plays	25.00	30.50	35.75	91.25
Entertainment totals	150.00	165.75	161.25	477.00
Health				
Health club dues	0.00	0.00	0.00	0.00
Insurance	85.00	85.00	85.00	255.00
Prescriptions	25.50	35.00	35.00	95.50
Over-the-counter drugs	24.26	40.16	15.62	80.04
Health totals	134.76	160.16	135.62	430.54
Personal				
Clothing	45.00	25.65	65.55	136.20
Salon/barber	35.00	45.00	40.00	120.00
Books	15.25	0.00	20.45	35.70
Music (CDs, etc.)	15.00	13.25	22.20	50.45
Personal totals	110.25	83.90	148.20	342.35
Financial obligations				
Long-term savings	0.00	0.00	0.00	0.00
Retirement (401k, Roth IRA)	0.00	0.00	0.00	0.00
Credit card payments	400.00	400.00	400.00	1,200.00
Other obligations	85.00	150.00	25.00	260.00
Financial obligation totals	485.00	550.00	425.00	1,460.00
Total expenses	3,651.29	3,471.45	3,583.13	10,710.87
Cash short/extra	423.96	629.05	502.32	1,550.33

Figure 4. Updated Smith Family Spending Plan, Continued

Adopt a More Frugal Lifestyle

With your expenses, debt and income addressed, turn your attention to living a more frugal life. Unfortunately, practicing frugality is too often translated as buying the least expensive products or services. Particularly in difficult economic times, there may be a tendency to make every effort to spend less no matter what. Blindly spending less is not frugal, it's cheap. Being frugal means spending money wisely in an attempt to get as much value from selected products and services as possible.

There is no doubt that discount stores and other low-cost options can be attractive; however, you have to be mindful of the fact that you often get what you pay for. It makes no sense to spend your hard-earned money on products or services that will not hold up, that will not stand the test of time. Does that mean that you should look to brand name products first? Not necessarily. Too often people overpay for products and services, basing their buying decisions on flashy advertisements and name recognition instead of thorough research and evaluation.

When conducting your research and evaluating different products and services to spend your hard-earned money on, you should consider these two factors first, quality and consistency. Quality is a more important factor than cost. If you pay $50 for a pair of jeans that last you two years, that is better than paying $20 for a pair of jeans of questionable quality that only last six months, after being washed a handful of times. Does buying the same pair of jeans four times ($80) over the course of two years make much sense when you can buy one pair of jeans for $50 that last as long? Of course not! When you spend your hard-earned money you want to be certain that the quality will be consistent from purchase to purchase. One potential benefit, one reason to consider name brand products and services, is that you can generally count on consistency. Whatever you think of McDonald's and its food, you can have a high level of confidence that a hamburger and fries purchased in November, in St. Louis, is going to taste the same as a hamburger and fries purchased in July, in San Francisco.

Put it all together and what does it mean? Being frugal does not mean automatically buying the least expensive good or service. Also, it certainly does not mean only considering name brand products or services, even though you might have a better idea of what to expect in terms of quality and consistency. Practicing frugality means taking the time to do your research to determine which products and services will give you the best bang for your buck; constantly evaluating if the products and services you normally buy are delivering quality on a consistent basis. There are times when that will mean buying the least expensive product or service and there will be occasions when that means buying a more expensive product or service that just happens to be a well-known brand.

Chapter Summary

Unfortunately, far too many American families are not fiscally fit and executing a coherent plan to secure their retirement. A significant number of families have no understanding, and no real desire, to learn more regarding saving and investing for their future, a number of families understand that they should be doing something, but are not sure where to start; and while some are saving and investing something, they are doing it blindly with no clear direction. Surveys such as those from the 2013 Retirement Confidence Survey (RCS) illustrate the numerous shortcomings with regards to the way in which Americans are preparing, or more accurately, not preparing for retirement.

Interestingly, numerous recent studies have shown that a majority of workers are planning to work past the age of 65, many are planning to work past age 70, and some have no plans to ever retire. The problem with that plan is that many of these workers may not have a choice but to leave the work force due to illness or injury; or it may simply be the case that the physical demands associated with their particular job may prevent them from staying as long as they would like to or need to. Additionally, if they are laid off from one job, they may find it is nearly impossible to get back into the work force in a meaningful way. Working longer is not the best plan. Developing and executing a solid retirement plan, and earlier done the better, is the most viable option.

The first step in the plan? Analyze your monthly expenses and develop a spending plan. Before you can determine how much money you can commit to savings and investments, you must determine how your money is currently being disbursed. The result of tracking your monthly expenses over a given time period will yield one of two results. Either your monthly income will exceed your monthly financial obligations or vice versa. In either case, particularly if your monthly obligations exceed your monthly income, you want to find every way possible to reduce your monthly expenses. The two most significant expenses in most families are related to housing and transportation. Look to trim the fat in those areas first. Additionally, credit card debt can be a significant burden. Plausible options for reducing credit card debt include requesting an interest rate reduction from the card issuer and seeking a credit card consolidation loan.

The yin to the yang of reducing expenses is increasing income. The first consideration should be to look no further than your current employer. Options there include asking for a raise, pursuing a promotion, volunteering for overtime, or volunteering for special assignments within your organization that offer proficiency/special duty pay. If no options exist within your present place of employment, consider outside options. If pride is an inhibitor, for your own good put it aside. There is absolutely no shame in picking up a second job at a supermarket, retailer, or restaurant for additional income. Remember, the income from any part-time job will go a long way toward helping reduce your monthly expenses and increasing the money available for funding your retirement accounts.

With your expenses reduced, your debt addressed and increased income if necessary, you should turn your attention to living a more frugal lifestyle. Be aware that being frugal does not mean automatically buying the least expensive good or service. Also, it certainly does not mean only considering name brand products or services, even though you might have a better idea of what to expect in terms of quality and consistency. Practicing frugality means taking the time to do your research to determine which products and services will give you the best bang for your buck; constantly evaluating if the products and services you normally buy are delivering quality on a consistent basis. There are times when that will mean buying the least expensive product or service and there will be occasions when that means buying a more expensive product or service that just happens to be a well-known brand.

As we continue the journey, we will revisit the Smiths in **Chapter 3**. There we will explore how they go about quantifying their retirement objectives and transitioning a spending plan that is currently focused on expenses, to one that ensures long-term retirement savings and investments are the focal points.

[2] CONDUCT PREPARATORY ACTIONS

Although I had brought my spending plan under control, I learned early on that nothing can be taken for granted and if I was not careful, my expenses could creep back up. Generally I was able to resist when the thought of buying a better this, or a newer that, crept into my consciousness. Once I worked my way into a position whereby my income exceeded my monthly financial expenses and I had money available to commit to savings and investments, I continued to find ways to whittle down my debt and longed to learn more about investment principles and practices that would enhance my chances for a comfortable retirement.

One of the first principles I came across was the value of establishing an emergency fund. In my reading I came across philosophies that suggested one year's living expenses; or three, six, or nine months of income among others. The one idea I came away with is that there are some key factors (e.g. level of job security, presence [or lack of] children, etc.) that could help to determine how to establish the requisite level of an emergency fund that was right for me. Considering the different philosophies detailing how much money should be accrued in an emergency fund and applying them to my own situation – secure employment in the U.S. Army being the factor that carried the most weight – I settled on the idea that four months of monthly expenses was adequate for my emergency fund.

While I did take a few college courses that touched on finance, the majority of what I learned was self-taught by reading every finance, investing, and retirement related publication I could get my hands on, visiting numerous finance and retirement related sites, and numerous conversations with some smart, savvy friends. As I learned more, I was able to combine new knowledge with my practical experiences and fine tune my retirement plan by effectively managing my spending plan, maintaining an appropriate emergency fund, continuing my education, and being attuned to factors such as understanding my potential Social Security benefits and understanding my credit report.

Work Your Spending Plan

Most people are familiar with the word *budget* and what it entails. Instead of budget, I prefer the term *spending plan.* While the two terms refer to the save activity - and I use them interchangeably - *budget* has many negative connotations. For many people, budget represents constraints and speaks to what they will not, or cannot, do. Conversely, a spending plan is viewed more favorably. It alludes to how money should flow in and out of your home; it helps you think in terms of what your values and goals are. If securing your family's financial future and preparing for retirement are important to you, it should be reflected in the way you spend your money.

Once your monthly expenses are reduced to the greatest extent possible, and you have identified the amount that can be committed to savings and investments, you are ready to work your spending plan, managing it as efficiently as possible. While the initial amount that is available for savings and investments will most likely not be enough to meet your retirement goal, it is a starting point.

By continually tracking, and limiting to the greatest extent possible, the amount of your income you are spending on debts, you will slowly be able to increase the amount available to commit to savings and investments and secure your retirement. In **Chapter 3** we will discuss how to determine what your monthly goal for savings and investments should be; and in **Chapter 5** we will discuss adjusting your spending plan and tracking your investments.

Establish an Emergency Fund

Simply put, an emergency fund is a cash account that is used only in the event of an emergency, to fill critical financial gaps, or meet unexpected expenses. It is immediate access to cash that allows you to take care of unforeseen circumstances without impacting the money you have committed to saving and investing. The account where your emergency fund is maintained should be one that offers the best yield possible. If given the choice between two institutions, one that pays .035 percent interest on a savings or checking account; or another that pays .10 percent, all other factors being equal, the choice is obvious.

While your current bank might be a good option, do not be afraid to look for alternatives. As an example, look to credit unions if you qualify for membership as they typically offer more attractive rates. Because they are not-for-profit organizations, they can take money that might otherwise be spent on things such as high salaries and feed it back to members. Take the time to do your research and identify your best option, keeping in mind that the most important factor is that the account should be easily accessible.

With respect to the question of how much should be maintained in an emergency fund, there are various schools of thought. While some suggest one year's living expenses, others suggest three, six, or nine months of income, while others might suggest something else entirely. A good friend of mine maintains one year's income in his emergency fund. In most cases, your marital status (theoretically single people should have more as they are reliant on a single income); the number of children in the household, and the level of job security are probably the primary factors. Other factors might be the age of your appliances, the age of your primary vehicle, as well as the age of other items in your household that might need repair or replacement. Ultimately, the amount will vary for everyone as the factors that impact their lives will be entirely different. However, I recommend three months living expenses as a minimum for your emergency fund.

Food for thought when determining the level of your emergency fund. While you certainly do not want to end up in a position where your emergency fund runs dry, it should be remembered that the more cash you have sitting in a low return account, the less money that is working for you. As touched on previously, you want to always be mindful of the power of compound interest which we will cover in greater detail in **Chapter 4**.

Educate Yourself

There are a number of ways that you can educate yourself about the ways in which the markets work, the differences between various investment products, how to acquire wealth, and how to prepare for retirement. I like to believe this book is a good start as it will go a long way to helping you construct a viable framework and get you focused on the factors that will determine your financial well-being. A useful tool within this book is the **Glossary of Terms** which will help you gain familiarization with common retirement and investment terms. However, I also encourage you to read finance related publications (e.g. The Wall Street Journal, Kiplinger), visit websites (e.g. CBS MoneyWatch), and blogs (e.g. RetirementSavvy.net); periodically watch finance related television channels (e.g. Bloomberg TV, CNBC); seek out finance and retirement related television specials and documentaries (a recent favorite of mine is *The Retirement Gamble* from PBS); and read reports/surveys that document the state of retirement for American families. As an example, those prepared by the Employee Benefit Research Institute (EBRI) and the Bureau of Labor Statistics (BLS) offer great insight.

As noted on their website, the mission of the EBRI® is to contribute to, encourage, and to enhance the development of sound employee benefit programs and sound public policy through objective research and education. They provide credible, reliable, and objective research, data, and analysis. Their annual Retirement Confidence Survey (RCS) highlights key retirement indicators. Sponsored by the EBRI, in conjunction with the American Savings Education Council (ASEC) and Mathew Greenwald & Associates (2014), the survey contains a core set of questions that is asked annually, allowing key attitudes and self-reported behavior patterns to be tracked over time. As part of their mission, the RCS strives to be timely by covering issues that are of current interest to policymakers and retirement benefits specialists. However, the great thing about the survey is that it is presented in such a way that lay people can easily follow the presentation and benefit from the insights.

Formal college level courses are also an education option. While I do not necessarily recommend that you enroll in college solely for the purpose of taking finance related classes, a great option is to take such courses as electives if you are already enrolled and engaged in a degree program. Unfortunately, personal finance classes are not as widespread as they should be; you will find that not every school offers these types of classes. However, that is starting to change as universities across the country are starting to realize the dangers of graduating students with significant debt and very little education with regards to understanding money and managing personal finances.

If you are fortunate to attend an institution that offers such classes, they will likely be entitled *"Personal Finance"* or something similar. The class should offer course work that deals with understanding money management concepts such as establishing values and goals, managing income, determining sources of income, preparing a spending plan, managing credit, understanding savings, understanding retirement plans, and providing for an adequate retirement.

By familiarizing yourself with finance and retirement related terminology, attaining formal education when possible, and educating yourself through engagement with multiple media sources, you will be better positioned to leverage readily information to enhance your retirement savings plan.

Understand Your Social Security Options

There is a lot of debate regarding the viability of Social Security program and its ability to pay out younger workers (particularly the Millennial Generation, those born from the early 1980 to the early 2000s) when they reach eligibility age. According to the Congressional Budget Office (2012), the trust fund will be exhausted in 2038 unless legislative action is taken. My belief is that legislative action will be taken in the intervening years and that

Social Security is a program that will be around for the foreseeable future. However, it is certainly possible, in fact probably likely, that the benefits structure will change by the time younger members of Generation X and Millennials are eligible to draw benefits.

With that said, you should understand that Social Security should not be the foundation of your retirement plan. While the Silent Generation and Baby Boomers have had the benefit of preparing for retirement comfortable in the knowledge that Social Security could play a significant role, that is not the case for the generations that have followed. The program and its benefits should be viewed as an augmentation to your personal savings and investments, particularly considering the likely coming changes. My suggestion is that you not get bogged down in the minutia of Social Security and worrying whether it will be around or not. At this point, you would be well served to simply understand how you earn Social Security benefits, regularly view your Social Security statement, and understand the different options, though they may change, for receiving benefits. I detail how to include Social Security benefits in your savings and investment plan in **Chapter 3**.

The basics of earning Social Security benefits are pretty straight forward. Your benefits will be based on three factors: the number of years you work, the number of credits you earn, and the average amount of money you earn each year. In order to qualify for retirement benefits, you will first need to earn 40 credits. The maximum number of credits that you can earn in one year is four. Therefore, you will need to work at least 10 years in order to qualify for Social Security retirement benefits. Once you have earned enough credits to qualify for retirement benefits, your estimated retirement benefits will be calculated.

A useful tool is the Social Security Benefit Statement. I recommend that you visit the Social Security Administration Website [http://www.ssa.gov/myaccount/] and register for a *my Social Security* account. There you can view your benefit statement as well as learn more about how the program works and your benefits. Two areas of interest on the benefit statement are the estimate of your retirement benefits and a history of your earnings. As you draw closer to retirement, you will need to decide when and how to start receiving your Social Security retirement benefits.

The most basic question revolves around receiving benefits earlier or later. If you live to the average life expectancy for someone your age, you will receive about the same amount in lifetime benefits no matter whether you choose to start receiving benefits at age 62, full retirement age, age 70, or any age in between. However, you should be aware that monthly benefit amounts can differ substantially based on your retirement age. Simply put, you can get lower monthly payments for a longer period of time or higher monthly payments over a shorter period of time. The amount you receive when you first get benefits sets the base for the amount you will receive for the rest of your life, though you do receive annual cost-of-living adjustments (COLA) regardless of when you start receiving your benefits.

To make the question of when and how to start receiving benefits a little more complicated, there are options for managing your Social Security benefits in such a way to increase them. By starting your benefits prior to full retirement age, stopping them at full retirement and then starting them up again at age 70, you will receive a greater amount based on the delayed retirement credit. Additionally, a spouse can claim a Social Security benefit based on their own earnings record or they can collect a spousal benefit that will provide 50% of the amount of their spouse's Social Security benefit as calculated at their full retirement age. Factors such as each spouse's earnings over the years will help to determine your best option.

However, as noted previously, it is best not to get too bogged down in the various ways in which you, and your spouse if married, can manage your benefits at this point. Ultimately, when and how you decide to receive your benefits will depend on numerous factors such as your marital status; how much you plan to receive from other sources (e.g. savings, IRAs, 401(k)s, pensions, annuities, etc.); and any legislative changes that might take place between the time you read this book and get close to your desired retirement age. Your best course of action is to visit the Social Security Administration Website [http://ssa.gov], your local Social Security Administration office, or visit a professional well versed in Social Security benefits when you get to the point of developing your nest-egg withdrawal plan. The rate, and order of withdrawal, will be discussed in greater detail in **Chapter 6**.

Check Your Credit Report

A good credit report, generally considered to be a score above 700, can be a valuable asset. Most significantly, with a better credit score you can get superior interest rates on house or car loans. Unfortunately, it is estimated that about 60% of information found on credit reports is either incorrect, outdated, or both. Considering that even the most seemingly insignificant errors can result in you paying a higher interest rate or cause you to be denied a loan completely, it is in your best interest to ensure that you check your credit report regularly for completeness and accuracy. Visit Annual Credit Report, this central site allows you to request a free credit report once every 12 months from each of the nationwide consumer credit reporting companies.

Once you receive your credit reports from the three credit bureaus – Experian™, Equifax®, and TransUnion® – start by checking your personal information such as Social Security number, the spelling of your name, current address, previous addresses, and date of birth for completeness and accuracy. Next, check your credit history. Ensure that the information (e.g. balance, credit limit, etc.) associated with each account is accurate and up to date. Check the status of your accounts. As examples, accounts that are *"closed"* or a loan that is *"paid in full"* should clearly be reflected on your report; and should show a zero balance. Negative remarks can be incredibly damaging. Look for words or phrases like *"collection"* or *"charged-off"* or statements indicating that a payment is late. If the information is not accurate, dispute the entry immediately and seek to have it removed or updated.

Next, check public record information. If your report shows a foreclosure, bankruptcy, foreclosure, tax lien or court judgment, ensure the information associated with the action is accurate. If it is not accurate, dispute the entry. Finally, check for any negative entries and their dates. Generally, negative information should be removed after seven years. If the information is older than seven years, take steps to have it removed. Each of the credit bureaus outlines how to go about disputing entries on their respective websites.

Chapter Summary

Once your monthly expenses are reduced to the greatest extent possible, and you have identified the amount that can be committed to savings and investments, you are ready to work your spending plan. Establishing an emergency fund should be your first step. The emergency fund is a cash account that is only used to fill critical financial gaps or to meet unexpected expenses. It is access to cash that allows you to take care of unforeseen circumstances without impacting the money you have committed to savings and investments. The next step is to educate yourself.

There are a number of ways that you can enlighten yourself about the differences between various investment products, how to acquire wealth, and how to prepare for retirement. Knowledge can be acquired by reading various finance publications, following various blogs, watching finance related television channels, and taking formal college level courses. A great option related to that last point is to take finance related classes as electives if you are already enrolled and engaged in a degree program. Look for classes entitled *"Personal Finance"* or something similar. The class should offer course work that deals with understanding money management concepts such as establishing values and goals, managing income, determining sources of income, preparing a spending plan, managing credit, understanding savings, understanding retirement plans, and providing for an adequate retirement. By familiarizing yourself with finance and retirement related terminology, enlightening yourself through engagement with multiple media sources, and attaining formal education when possible, you will be better positioned to leverage readily available information to enhance your retirement savings plan.

Though it is likely to change, I believe that Social Security will be around for the foreseeable future, and therefore, should be taken into consideration when making your retirement plans. Remember however, that it should not be the centerpiece of your plan. While the most basic question revolves around receiving benefits earlier or later, there are numerous other considerations such as your marital status, how much you plan to receive from other sources (e.g. savings, IRAs, 401(k)s, pensions, annuities, etc.), and any legislative changes that might take place over the years. Your best course of action is to visit the Social Security Administration's website, your local Social Security Administration office, or visit a professional well versed in Social Security benefits as you get closer to the point of developing your nest-egg withdrawal plan.

An additional step to take as you develop your retirement plan includes maintaining a good credit report. Get a copy of your credit report from each of the three credit reporting agencies and check your credit report regularly; focusing on the accuracy of your personal information, your credit history, and public record information. Dispute any inaccuracies immediately and work to remove any negative entries, if possible, that are more than seven years old. Your objective should be to maintain a credit score above 700. With a better credit score you put yourself in a position to get better interest rates on big ticket purchases such as a house or car loan.

[3] DETERMINE GOALS

When I first made up my mind to get fiscally fit, I had no idea what I desired in terms of an annual income in retirement. That determination would come later. Initially, I was more focused on simply getting my debt under control, finding money to commit to savings and investments, and educating myself on becoming a savvy investor. As I did those things and eventually started giving thought to what I desired in terms of an annual income in retirement, I came across different philosophies regarding how to establish that number. The philosophies for how to establish the number were often based on the idea that it should be some percentage (typically 70% or 80%) of your current household income.

Initially I utilized 80% as my guide, which adjusted my desired annual retirement income upward as my own salary increased and again when I got remarried and our household income increased. Ultimately I settled on the idea that 80% of my household income was not going to be enough due to numerous factors including the retirement lifestyle I desired, the anticipation that many costs (e.g. health care) will be higher than suspected, and a desire to assist family members if necessary. Over the years my number has continued to drift upward. Not only because of those factors, but the idea that nothing is lost if I shoot for a higher target, but happen to fall a little short. I would rather shot for an annual retirement income of $200,000 and miss, maybe ending up with $175,000, than aim for $100,000 annual retirement income and hit. Today, my wife and I are planning on having 105% of our current household income in retirement and are ahead of pace.

Quantify Retirement Objectives

Now that your monthly expenses are under control – with the understanding that you should continually search for ways to reduce them even more – and you have conducted preparatory actions, you are ready to establish your nest-egg goal, and specify what you need to do to reach that number. That will be achieved by performing a retirement needs calculation.

While we will be discussing lots of numbers – including the number of years until you plan to retire and rate of return on your investments among others - our primary focus will be on what I call the four big numbers: the percentage of your current annual household income you hope to maintain in retirement, your nest-egg goal, the 4% rule, and monthly contributions.

Ultimately the question is, *"how much do I need to save and invest on a monthly basis during my working years to reach my desired nest-egg and have a comfortable retirement?"* As we discussed previously, most of us operate on a monthly basis with regard to receiving income and meeting our financial obligations, whether they be household expenses, car expenses, paying credit cards, or funding retirement plans. The first three factors will help us zero in on the fourth factor, how much to save on a monthly basis.

As I touched on when discussing my story, there are numerous philosophies regarding how to determine your annual income in retirement. They all basically revolve around the idea that your retirement income should be some percentage of your current household income. There really is no correct percentage as this is a very personal choice and there are any number of factors (e.g. desired lifestyle, anticipated health care costs, plans for providing an inheritance to children/grandchildren, etc.) that each individual/couple will have to take into consideration. As an initial percentage (it can always be adjusted later) I recommend that you start with at least 75% of your current household income. Keeping that number in the back of our minds, next we look at the 4% rule.

The rule was developed in the mid-1990s by William Bengen, A Southern California financial planner, as a tool for advisers in helping their clients. Basically the rule says that if you take out 4% of your nest-egg the first year in retirement, and then adjust that rate to account for inflation in each subsequent year (e.g. if inflation rises 1% during your first year of retirement, you would withdraw 5% of your nest-egg during your second year in retirement), you will not run out of money for at least three decades. This calculation is based on historical returns for an investor with a portfolio comprised of 60% large company stocks and 40% bonds. While there is some doubt about the veracity of the rule – some believe it is simply too arbitrary, some believe it is too high, and some believe too low – it provides a good starting point.

Using our favorite family, the Smiths, as an example, we will use the 75% philosophy and 4% rule to determine their retirement nest-egg. Looking at the income of $12,261.20 (**Figure 3**) they reported over the course of three months when they were doing their spending plan, we will extend that over the course of a full year which gives us $49,044 as their current household annual income. Keeping it simple, let's round that up to $50,000. Applying the 75% philosophy to $50,000 (50,000 x .75) we get $37,500. This is the amount they can draw from their nest-egg annually in retirement.

Taking that number, $37,500, and applying the 4% rule (37,500/.04) we get $937,500. This is the nest-egg that they must have when they retire to give themselves a reasonable level of confidence that they can withdraw $37,500 annually without worry of running out of money for 30 years. Those are a lot of numbers to deal with. A recap:

Current Annual Household Income = $50,000
Annual Income Desired in Retirement Applying the 75% Philosophy = $37,500 (50,000 x .75)
Required Nest-Egg Applying the 4% Rule = $937,500 (37,500/.04)

That takes care of the first three big numbers which leaves the last, monthly contributions required to get to the nest-egg number. As you continue to educate yourself about personal finance and retirement, one phrase you are likely to hear is that retirement planning is *one part science and one part art.* This is based on the idea that while some things are rooted in mathematical fact (e.g. 50,000 x .75 = 37,500) and will not change, some of the elements in your calculations (e.g. rate you will earn on your returns or number of years you will be working to build your nest-egg) are unknowable or subject to change. That is one reason why I suggest you aim high (e.g. perhaps 90% of your current income as retirement income vice 75%) but use conservative calculations (6% vice 12% as a rate of return).

We have now reached one point where we combine science and art and we try to determine the last of the big four numbers, the monthly contributions you will have to make to reach your desired nest-egg. At this point you will need a good compound interest calculator. My personal favorite can be found at the Moneychimp® website [http://moneychimp.com]. ***Note:*** *For the following examples, I utilized the "Make Additions at the Start of Each Compounding Period" option.*

The numbers we will plug into the calculator include Current Principal (money currently in savings and investments accounts) Annual Addition, Years to Grow (number of years before you plan to retire), and Interest Rate (what you hope to earn on your investments). Using the calculator at Moneychimp, or any similar compound interest calculator, we plug in our numbers.

Let's make a few of assumptions about our fictional family, the Smiths. First, even though they are not currently contributing to any retirement accounts, we will assume they were at one time and have $17,500 between them in IRA accounts. Second, going back and referencing their Updated Family Spending Plan (**Figure 4**), you will recall that after reducing some of their expenses, their average monthly surplus is $516.78. For our purposes, we will reduce that to a nice even $500 that is available to commit to savings and investments. Third, let's assume they are both 30 years old and would like to retire at 60, which gives them 30 years to build their nest-egg.

A quick side note. This number really is part of the *'art'* of investing we touched on earlier. No one knows for certain what their rate of return will be over any given time period and if you research *'historical rates of return'* you will find the results of many studies that look at different time periods, different investment vehicles, and many other factors to arrive at different numbers. One of the first proclamations I heard when first conducting my own research was that the stock market has returned ~10% during every recorded twenty year period since 1910 or so. If you search for 15 minutes on the Internet, you are likely to find a wide range of proclamations regarding what the market has historically returned. For planning purposes, we will assume the Smith's rate of return will be 6%. A recap of the Smith's numbers thus far:

Current Annual Household Income = $50,000
Annual Income Desired in Retirement Applying the 75% Philosophy = $37,500 (50,000 x .75)
Required Nest-Egg Applying the 4% Rule = $937,500 (37,500/.04)
Current Principal = $17,500
Annual Addition = $6,000 (500 x 12)
Years to Grow = 30
Interest Rate = 6%

INPUTS	
CURRENT PRINCIPAL	$17,500
ANNUAL ADDITION	$6,000
YEARS TO GROW	30
INTEREST RATE	6%
RESULT	
FUTURE VALUE	$603,321.16

Figure 5. Nest-Egg Calculation: Initial

Plugging the numbers into our compound interest calculator, we see that the Future Value of their nest-egg would be $603,321.16 (**Figure 5**). Of course that number is short of their $937,500 goal. At this point, we apply more of the art we talked about previously to see how some changes to our calculations impact that Future Value number. First, what happens if the Smiths work harder at reducing their monthly expenses, freeing up another $150/month for savings and investments? Now instead of an Annual Addition of $6,000, that number increases to $7,800.

INPUTS	
CURRENT PRINCIPAL	$17,500
ANNUAL ADDITION	$7,800
YEARS TO GROW	30
INTEREST RATE	6%
RESULT	
FUTURE VALUE	$754,164.18

Figure 6. Nest-Egg Calculation: Adjusted Annual Addition

Making that change in our calculator, we see that the Smiths are now looking at a $754,164.18 nest-egg (**Figure 6**). Keeping the other factors the same, what happens if they agree to work two additional years, until age 62? Plugging in the new number we see that the Smiths are now looking at a $864,410.95 nest-egg (**Figure 7**). Still a little short of their goal.

Keeping the other factors the same, if the Smiths are able to achieve just a .5% increase in the Interest Rate (what they earn on their investments sans fees, etc.), we see that they have now exceeded their goal with a $962,266.68 nest-egg (**Figure 8**). To arrive at what the Smiths would need to contribute on a monthly basis we simply divide that Annual Addition number, $7,800 in this case, by 12.

INPUTS	
CURRENT PRINCIPAL	$17,500
ANNUAL ADDITION	$7,800
YEARS TO GROW	32
INTEREST RATE	6%
RESULT	
FUTURE VALUE	$864,410.95

Figure 7. Nest-Egg Calculation: Adjusted Years to Grow

INPUTS	
CURRENT PRINCIPAL	$17,500
ANNUAL ADDITION	$7,800
YEARS TO GROW	32
INTEREST RATE	6.5%
RESULT	
FUTURE VALUE	$962,266.68

Figure 8. Nest-Egg Calculation: Adjusted Interest Rate

For the Smiths, in this scenario they would need to contribute $650 monthly. Their bottom line numbers:

Current Annual Household Income = $50,000
Annual Income Desired in Retirement Applying the 75% Philosophy = $37,500 (50,000 x .75)
Required Nest-Egg Applying the 4% Rule = $937,500 (37,500/.04)
Current Principal = $17,500
Annual Addition = $7,800 (650 x 12)
Years to Grow = 32
Interest Rate = 6.5%

At this point, I think it should be clear that while some things (e.g. knowing exactly how your investments will perform during any given year) are out of your control, there are a lot of factors (e.g. reducing expenses to increase savings and investments, making adjustments to the size of your desired net-egg, the number of years you work, etc.) that you can control. Being fiscally fit means being acutely aware of the things within your control, taking charge of them, and managing them in such a way as to increase your chances of reaching your retirement goals.

Transition Your Spending Plan

With your monthly contribution number in mind, you can now turn your attention to transitioning your spending plan. Running the calculation the first few times is not the end of the story, it is really only the beginning. Those are not the numbers you will be working with during the entire period you are building your nest-egg. The initial calculations are simply a way for you to gauge where you are at the beginning of this process relative to where you want to be. Moreover, do not get discouraged - or let others discourage you - if your target nest-egg number seems out of reach. We will discuss some factors that will impact that number later, in **Chapter 5**. For now, just recognize that you must transition your spending plan from one that was largely focused on monthly expenses to one that is focused on long-term savings and retirement accounts. Adjustments (e.g. salary increases, expenses decreased, modified goals, etc.) to your spending plan will be made over time.

Chapter Summary

Now that your monthly expenses are under control and you have conducted preparatory actions, you are ready to establish your nest-egg goal and specify what you need to do to reach that number. That will be achieved by performing a retirement needs calculation. While we discussed lots of different numbers, the key numbers are the percentage of your current annual household income you hope to maintain in retirement, your nest-egg goal, the 4% rule, and your monthly contributions. Ultimately the question is, *"how much do I need to save/invest on a monthly basis during my working years to reach my desired nest-egg and have a comfortable retirement?"*

The RWR Retirement Planner is a comprehensive tool that captures all of the information required to develop your nest-egg number, makes it easy to track progress, make adjustments, and view all relevant retirement numbers on one easily read and understood spreadsheet. Having a prepared worksheet will be beneficial later as we will cover making adjustments to your plan and tracking your investments in greater detail in **Chapter 5**.

[4] INVEST

My first retirement account, established in the summer of 2001, was a Roth IRA account. I chose to open the account myself, online, with a financial services company vice opening it through a financial product salesperson. Not only did I have access to a wide range of investment options (e.g. mutual funds, exchange traded funds [ETFs], a brokerage account, IRAs, etc.), I avoided unnecessary fees that would negatively impact my rate of return. Because I had cut back on my monthly expenses and increased my income, I was able to maximize the contributions ($2,000 was the limit in 2001) to my Roth IRA.

Unfortunately, at that time the Thrift Savings Plan (TSP) – the defined contribution plan for federal civil service employees which utilizes the same rules as 401(k)s – was not offered to active duty service members. Fortunately however, soon after I began seriously focusing on building my nest-egg, the TSP was opened up to active duty service members and I took advantage of the opportunity. While I was not in a position at that time to maximize contributions, that would soon change.

Upon my retirement from active duty toward the end of 2005, I was steadily improving my fiscal fitness and excited about securing a position as a Department of the Army Civilian. The increased salary, along with my new pension, put me in a position to really step up my contributions. Not only was I able to continue to maximize contributions to my Roth IRA, it was not long before I was able to maximize contributions to the TSP also. I maintained that course without disruption for a couple of years.

By the time I retired in 2005, I had started dating Karen, who would later become my wife. As our relationship became more serious and we began discussing money and finance, it was revealed that while she was not carrying significant debt, she also was not focused on planning for retirement. That soon changed. While she did have a small amount of money in her TSP account, she had no other saving or investment accounts to speak of. One afternoon I encouraged her to sit down and open an IRA account online, just as I had done years before.

While she was not able to purchase a mutual fund right away - many require a minimum amount (e.g. $2,500) for the initial purchase - to her credit she opened the account and consistently made monthly contributions, even though it was often financially difficult. The great thing about institutions such as Fidelity is that even though you may not have the minimum amount to purchase a mutual fund right away, they will allow you to open the account and park your contributions in a money market account which you can fund on a recurring basis and/or make periodic contributions. Once you accrue the minimum investment amount in the money market account, you can then select and purchase the fund of your choice.

Such was the case with Karen and her Roth IRA Account. It was not too long before she had enough to meet the minimum requirement and invested in her first mutual fund, a lifecycle fund. As she crossed that minimum threshold to buy the lifecycle fund and watched her balance slowly grow, Karen became much more interested in understanding her investments and focused on securing a comfortable retirement.

As our relationship became more serious, there was a slight disruption to my full throttled contributions - which was not a bad thing - as we decided to buy a home and marry. The purchase of a new home, and all the expenses that go with it, forced me to reduce my contributions somewhat for a couple of years. However, early on in our marriage Karen and I agreed that we would both work to put ourselves in a position to maximize contributions to both our Roth IRA accounts and TSP accounts. By slowly increasing our monthly contributions whenever we received raises and/or reduced debt, we were able to reach our goal within a few years.

The Power of Compound Interest

It is widely reported, or rumored, that Albert Einstein once made an observation along the lines that the most powerful force in the universe is compound interest or that compound interest is the greatest mathematical discovery of all time. Whether Einstein said either, or something similar, we may never know. However, what we do know is that interest, when compounded, is probably the most significant factor with regards to growing your nest-egg.

Perhaps the easiest way to communicate the phenomenon is with the story of two brothers. Let's assume Robert Smith, the husband in our fictional family, has a twin brother named Ronald Smith. When the twins were 28 years old, they had a conversation regarding savings and investments. Ronald noted that he had managed to reduce his debt and was prepared to invest $1,000 a year. Robert noted, regrettably, that he had not been able to reduce his debt and was not in a position to invest any of his income. Flash forward seven years and the twins are now 35 years old. Ronald has been investing $1,000 faithfully during that time, earned 10%

annually on his investments and is now sitting on a $10,435.89 portfolio (**Figure 9**). During the previous seven years, Robert was not able to invest anything. Fortunately however, he is now at the point where he is able and prepared to invest $1,000 annually. While Robert is just now starting to invest, Ronald decides that he is no longer interested in contributing new money to his investment accounts. Not something that I would recommend, but it makes the point more dramatic. Fortunately however, he does decide to leave the $10,435.89 in place. Over their birthday dinner last Tuesday, the twins both expressed a desire to retire at 60 years of age, in 25 years.

Summarized, Ronald invested $1,000 a year for seven years, left the resultant $10,435.89 in place, but has decided to stop investing new money for the next 25 years. His total contributions: $7,000. Conversely, Robert did not invest any money during the seven years that his brother did; however, he did start contributing to his retirement accounts at the same time his brother stopped, deciding to faithfully contribute $1,000 annually for the next 25 years. His total contributions: $25,000. Which brother do you believe will have a larger nest-egg when they celebrate their 60th birthday?

INPUTS	
CURRENT PRINCIPAL	$0
ANNUAL ADDITION	$1,000
YEARS TO GROW	7
INTEREST RATE	10%
RESULT	
FUTURE VALUE	$10,435.89

Figure 9. Ronald Smith: Ages 28-35

INPUTS	
CURRENT PRINCIPAL	$10,135.89
ANNUAL ADDITION	$0
YEARS TO GROW	25
INTEREST RATE	10%
RESULT	
FUTURE VALUE	$113,069.80

Figure 10. Ronald Smith: Ages 35-60

INPUTS	
CURRENT PRINCIPAL	$0
ANNUAL ADDITION	$1,000
YEARS TO GROW	25
INTEREST RATE	10%
RESULT	
FUTURE VALUE	$108,181.77

Figure 11. Robert Smith: Ages 35-60

As you probably suspected, even though he contributed $18,000 less, Ronald Smith (**Figure 10**) will have a larger nest-egg (+ $4,888.03) than his brother, Robert (**Figure 11**). It is likely that as you conduct your research and learn more, you will come across different versions of this story. Regardless of the slight differences, the truth is the same. By putting your money to work as soon as possible – and limiting negative impacts such as fees paid to *'expert'* advisors – the power of compound interest can work for you. That is why when someone states that they cannot afford to invest at the moment; I implore them to find a way, because they cannot afford not to invest right now. Starting early is critical. Saving for retirement should be happening regardless of where you are in the continuum of your career, your working life.

Every day that your money is not working for you is a lost opportunity, a slight dampening of your retirement prospects. One of the *secrets* to acquiring wealth and successfully preparing for retirement is to recognize the power of compound interest. It is nearly impossible to have an earned income that can match the power of portfolio income. While a $30, $40, or $50 per hour job sounds nice, and it is, it pales in comparison to having $30,000, $40,000, or $50,000 earning returns for you while you are working the 8 to 5. The key is that you first have to lower your debt and free up money to fund your savings and investment accounts. We will discuss earned income and portfolio income – along with passive income – in greater detail later, in **Chapter 7**.

Now is probably a good time to address utilizing professional advisors as I touched on them briefly, earlier. Financial advisors generally fall into one of three categories: money managers, product salespeople, and financial planners. Money managers attempt to grow the portfolio under their management, funds from numerous investors, and invest in some sector of the market in which they believe they have particular expertise that will allow them to generate higher rates of return than individuals can attain on their own. Of course their clients are expected to pay a premium for that expertise. Product salespeople often focus on selling clients a narrow range of products that come with high fees. Unfortunately, they typically place their own agenda, or that of their company, ahead of their client's. I recommend you avoid these advisors.

Finally, there are the financial planners. These individuals take a comprehensive view of their client's finances, considers their goals, and help them develop a plan to meet those goals while considering tax saving and various investment strategies. Should you decide you require, or desire, the services of a professional, your best bet is this type of advisor. There are a few different flavors of planners and lots of acronyms.

From Certified Financial Planners (CFP), to Chartered Financial Consultants (ChFC), to Certified Financial Analysts (CFA), to Personal Financial Analysts, you certainly have lots of choices. While it might seem as if it would be impossible to choose one vice another, the bottom line is that each of these professionals generally focuses on one or more of the following areas: insurance, taxes, retirement, and estate planning. If considering a financial planner or any type of advisor, pay close attention to the fee structure. I recommend one that has a fair amount of experience, has attained some sort of certification, and the fee is based on a flat hourly rate vice a percentage of your portfolio value. Additionally, seek a planner that focuses on your area(s) of interest and seems most interested in working with you to advance your goals as opposed to their own. Do not be afraid to ask as many questions as you feel necessary to be comfortable. Remember, it is your money that you will be spending for their services. If they will not answer, or seem reluctant to answer some of your questions, walk away. Quickly.

There will likely come a time when finding a good planner is appropriate. As an example, a friend of mine recently started consulting with a professional advisor as he and his wife are within a few years of retiring should they choose. While he is comfortable with the decisions he has made at this point and given significant thought to his withdrawal plan (a topic covered in great detail in **Chapter 6**), he would like to get a second opinion to ensure he has not overlooked anything or is not considering pertinent information. Similarly, I plan to do the same thing when I get to within four or five years of retiring. While I have the broad outlines of a withdrawal plan in mind, I recognize that there may be factors that I have missed, or not fully considered, and a second opinion might prove valuable.

Retirement Savings Plans

There are two major types of employee retirement savings plans: defined benefit and defined contribution. A defined benefit plan, funded by the employer, promises you a specific monthly benefit at retirement. The plan may state the promised benefit as an exact dollar amount, such as $600 per month at retirement. More often however, the benefit is calculated through a formula that includes factors such as the employee's salary, their age, and the number of years they worked at the company. For example, a company's pension benefit might be equal to 1.5% of an employee's average salary for the last three years of employment times their total years of service. If an employee worked for a company for 30 years and their average salary over the last three years was $55,529, their defined pension would be $24,988.05 (55,529 x .015 x 30) annually or $2,082.34 monthly. Unfortunately, the defined benefit plan is becoming a rarity.

As noted by William J. Wiatrowski (2012), only 10% of all private sector establishments provided defined benefit plans, covering 18% of private industry employees in 2011; and that decline in pension coverage over the past 30 years is a function of two simultaneous trends: a decline in coverage among all workers and a shift in employment toward those groups of workers with less coverage. For example, among larger private establishments in 1993, 81% of full-time union employees had pension coverage while only 48% of their nonunion counterparts had such coverage.

Similarly, among smaller private establishments in 1994, pensions covered 72% of full-time union workers and 12% of full-time nonunion workers. Combined, the proportion with pension coverage was nearly three times greater among full-time union workers than among full-time nonunion workers (76% compared to 28%). However, today those ratios are much different. Although the proportion with pension coverage has declined for both union and nonunion workers, the decline has been greater for nonunion workers. In 2011, 67% of union workers had pension coverage (down from 76%, a 12% drop). Among nonunion workers, 13% had coverage, which is down from 28%, a 54% drop.

The bottom line is that landscape has been shifting for quite some time for all workers. Since 1998, employers have been steadily shifting their retirement offerings for newly hired salaried employees away from traditional defined benefit plans. At the end of 1998, 90% of Fortune 100 companies offered a defined contribution plan and some sort of defined benefit plan, either a traditional or hybrid (account-based pension, typically cash balance) plan. Today only 30% of the Fortune 100 companies offer a defined benefit plan to their new salaried hires. Offering defined contribution benefits only has become a prevalent practice (Towers Watson, 2012).

Unfortunately, the news only gets worse. A relatively recent phenomenon among private industry employers still offering defined benefit plans is '*frozen plans.*' When plans are frozen, they are closed to new employees and disturbingly, some frozen plans even stop accruing benefits for current employees. The Bureau of Labor Statistics began capturing information on frozen defined benefit plans in 2009, when one in five participants were in such a plan. By 2011, that figure had increased to one in four participants. The result? Because frozen plans are closed to new employees, as current employees retire or otherwise leave the plan and new employees are hired, the percentage of workers covered by these plans will continue to decline over time (Wiatrowski, 2012).

A defined contribution plan, on the other hand, does not promise an employee a specific benefit amount at retirement. Instead, the employee and/or the employer contribute money to the employee's individual account in the plan. In many cases, the employees are responsible for choosing how these contributions are invested, and deciding how much to contribute from their paycheck through pretax deductions. The employer may add to the employee's account, in some cases by matching a certain percentage of their contributions.

The value of the employee's account depends on how much is contributed and how well the investments perform. At retirement, the employee receives the balance in their account, reflecting the contributions, investment gains or losses, and any fees charged against their account. What does all this mean? As the defined benefit plan drifts away, slowly being replaced by the defined contribution plan, it means that you are largely on your own with regards to funding your retirement. However, that does not have to be a bad thing. If you educate yourself, and take charge of your finances by developing a comprehensive plan and actively tracking your results, a comfortable retirement is well within your reach.

The traditional 401(k) plan is the most popular type of defined contribution plan. However, there are other types as well: safe harbor 401(k), SIMPLE 401k, and automatic enrollment 401(k) plans. The SIMPLE IRA plan, SEP, employee stock ownership plan (ESOP), and profit sharing plan are other examples of defined contribution plans (United States Department of Labor, ND). However, for most employees, it is likely that the traditional 401(k) will be the plan available to them and the centerpiece of their retirement accounts. The maximum employee contribution permitted to 401(k) plans in 2013 is $17,500. Fortunately, the IRS periodically raises the maximum contribution limit to these plans. Additionally, the IRS provides an opportunity for older workers to better position themselves in retirement through catch-up contributions for workers over 50. For those that qualify, an additional $5,500 can be contributed starting in the year they turn 50.

There are two major types of individual retirement savings plans, the traditional Individual Retirement Account (IRA) and the Roth IRA. Like the 401(k), the IRS periodically raises the maximum contribution limit.

During the 2008 – 2012 period, the limit was $5,000. In 2013 the limit was raised to $5,500 per year. And also, just like the 401(k), IRAs allow for catch-up contributions for those over 50 years of age. For 2013, that limit is $1,000. With a traditional IRA, contributions are taken off of your yearly income, which has the effect of lowering your total tax liability for that year. However, once funds in an IRA are withdrawn, they are subject to standard income taxes and an additional 10% penalty if the funds are withdrawn before the age of 59½.

Unlike traditional IRAs, Roth IRAs are not tax-deductible. However, the contributions to a Roth IRA can be withdrawn at any time without being subject to a penalty. Interest earned on the account, however, is subject to a penalty or tax. After five years, contributions and earnings in the account can be withdrawn without penalty or taxation. Be aware that there are limits to contributing to a Roth IRA if your modified Adjusted Gross Income (AGI) is above a certain level. Generally, for married couples, limits start to kick in at $173,000 and your ability to contribute ends once your AGI hits $183,000. For single filers, the numbers are $110,000 and $125,000 respectively. As these numbers are always subject to change and there may be other factors, I recommend that you visit the IRS Publication 590 Webpage for the official rules. An option for a quick check is Moneychimp, which has a Roth IRA Income and Contribution Limit calculator.

Just as there are rules regarding contributions to retirement plans, there are IRS rules, known as Required Minimum Distributions (RMD), that mandate when savings must be drawn down from most retirement accounts. We will discuss the RMD in greater detail in **Chapter 6**.

Start Contributions to Retirement Plans

If you are one of the increasingly few that is with an employer that offers a defined benefit plan, a pension, you are in an enviable position. You are in a position to get off to a great start simply by virtue of working for a particular employer. For everyone however, those employed by an organization that offers a pension or not, the time has come to start contributing to your retirement plans. Your first action should be to contribute to a 401(k) if your employer offers a defined contribution plan. Working on the assumption you will not initially be in a position to maximum your contributions ($17,500 in 2013) you should invest as much as possible, or at least enough to earn your employer's matching contributions, if they offer a plan.

The way matching works is fairly straight forward. As an example, assume an employer offers a 50/5 plan. That means they will match up to 50% on the first 5%; which means that your employer will place 50 cents into your retirement plan for every dollar you put in; and each year, there is a limit of 5% of your gross salary that the employer will match. As an example, an individual with a salary of $75,000 that contributes at least 5% to her 401(k) plan will receive a matching contribution from the employer of $1,875 (75,000 / 2 x .05). If your employer is offering to give you an additional $1,875 a year, why would you pass it up? Answer. You should not. Free money is a good thing. A very good thing indeed!

Whatever your situation - whether you are fortunate enough to be in a position where you can maximize your 401(k) contributions, you are able to contribute something to your 401(k), but less than the maximum, or your employer does not offer a 401(k) plan – your next action should be to establish an IRA account. I prefer the Roth IRA for the tax advantages at the time of withdrawal. Even if you are not able to make large or regular contributions to your accounts, I strongly encourage you to participate in the 401(k) if you have the opportunity and to open an IRA account as soon as possible.

As touched on previously, I recommend that you open and manage your own IRA account vice going through a product salesperson. Opening your own IRA account with a professional, reputable, low-fee company such as Fidelity® or Vanguard® is incredibly easy and will save you money, money that should be working for you. You should open the account once you have conducted some research and found a company that offers services (IRAs, brokerage account, etc.) that might be of interest to you, and do so at reasonable rates. You will find that creating an account is easy and can be done within a few minutes online.

With regards to how to fund your 401(k) and your IRA, you are going to have to take some time to study the various options. As you might expect, the mutual fund universe is comprised of a diverse, large number of companies. Typically however, organizations that offer 401(k)s provide the plans through a small, perhaps even a single, number of companies. Therefore, the choice will be easier as you will be limited in the number of mutual funds to choose from. My advice is that you keep it simple and stick with index mutual funds. A quick primer on mutual funds. A mutual fund is essentially a company that pools money from many investors and invests the money in stocks, bonds, short-term money-market instruments, other securities or assets, or some combination of these different investments. The combined holdings the mutual fund owns are known as its portfolio. Each share represents an investor's proportionate ownership of the fund's holdings and the income those holdings generate.

An index fund is a specific type of mutual fund. These types of mutual funds are designed to track the performance of a stock market index (e.g. Russell 2000, S&P 500, Wilshire 5000, NASDAQ Composite, etc.). Advantages of these types of funds is that they offer investors broad exposure to the markets and most importantly, expenses that are typically lower than traditional mutual funds due to their passive, vice active, management.

Regarding expenses, I recommend that you seek funds that have an expense ratio (the operating costs, including management fees, expressed as a percentage of the fund's average net assets for a given time period) that is less than 1%. As we have discussed previously, the more money you have working for you, and not going to fees and other expenses, they more you can leverage the power of compound interest.

It would behoove you to conduct due diligence and understand both the upsides and the downsides of mutual fund investing and how to choose the fund(s) that match your goals and tolerance for risk. As you conduct your research, remember that past performance is not a reliable indicator of future performance. While past performance can help you assess a fund's volatility over time, do not become too enamored by the previous year's returns. In the case of investing, the past is not necessarily prologue.

Another good option, which is relatively new, is lifecycle funds. Lifecycle funds are an easy way to manage investments during your working years. They consist of a series of target retirement date funds in five or ten-year increments and you select the fund nearest your anticipated retirement date. The underlying idea of lifecycle funds is that they are low-cost, as the management is fairly passive (like index funds), and their weighting with regards to equities and bonds; and volatility and risk are adjusted to become more conservative as you get closer to the target date, near your date of retirement.

Take the time to learn as much as possible about index mutual funds, lifecycle funds, and the following terms/topics: exchange traded funds (ETFs), expense ratios, diversification, asset allocation, dollar cost averaging, dividends, portfolio rebalancing, and asset class. There are many more terms/topics you will come across, but these should be a good start and will help you with determining which instruments to use in funding your retirement accounts. The **Glossary of Terms** at the end of this book provides some useful terms and definitions.

Pay Yourself First

There really is not a great deal to be said with regards to this idea. Now that you have done some research and educated yourself; lowered your monthly expenses (and perhaps increased your income), freeing up money for investments; developed a workable spending plan; established your retirement goals; established your retirement accounts; and determined the instruments you will use to fund those accounts, you are ready to begin paying yourself.

Not only should you now be ready to pay yourself, you should be ready to pay yourself first. Prior to paying your bills, eating out, and spending money on entertainment, pay yourself! This is made easier as your 401(k) contributions will be automatically deducted from your paycheck and any company you establish your IRA with will have an option for automatic withdrawals from your checking account. I strongly encourage you to take advantage of this capability. You will find that if you never see the money, you will not miss it.

In fact, you should strive to automate all of your finances. Everything from getting paid, funding investment/savings accounts, and paying bills should be done via automatic deductions and payments. Moreover, you should leverage the Internet as it allows you to view the status of your accounts, conduct your financial related activities (e.g. view account balances, make additional payments, etc.) at your convenience, and manage your financial life in a real-time, efficient manner. The rise of the Internet over the last 15 years and its ability to deliver relevant information, in real-time when necessary, and as a medium for comparing investment options has made portfolio management a realistic option for individual investors.

Chapter Summary

It is said that Albert Einstein, a pretty smart fella, once made an observation along the lines that the most powerful force in the universe is compound interest or that compound interest is the greatest mathematical discovery of all time. Whether Einstein said either, or something similar, we may never know. However, what we do know is that interest, when compounded, is probably the most significant factor with regards to growing your nest-egg.

Combined with time, compound interest is the factor that can have the most profound impact on growing your nest-egg. To grow that nest-egg, you will likely rely on one or both of the two major types of employee retirement savings plans: defined benefit and defined contribution; and one of the two types (traditional IRA or Roth IRA) of individual retirement savings plans. The employee retirement savings plan, a defined benefit plan, is funded by the employer, and promises you a specific monthly benefit at retirement. Normally that benefit is calculated through a formula that includes factors such as your salary, your age, and the number of years you worked at the company.

Unfortunately, employers have been steadily shifting their retirement offerings for newly hired salaried employees away from traditional defined benefit plans. At the end of 1998, 90% of Fortune 100 companies offered a defined contribution plan and some sort of defined benefit plan, either a traditional or hybrid (account-based pension, typically cash balance) plan. Today only 30% of the Fortune 100 companies offer a defined benefit plan to their new salaried hires. Offering defined contribution benefits only has become a prevalent practice (Towers Watson, 2012). There is no reason to suspect that companies will shift back to defined benefit plans. That ship has definitely sailed. That means that individuals need to take more responsibility for themselves through the use of defined contribution and individual retirement plans.

Defined contribution plans do not promise you a specific benefit amount at retirement. Instead, you and/or your employer contribute money to your individual account in the plan. In many cases, you are responsible for choosing how these contributions are invested, and deciding how much to contribute from your paycheck through pretax deductions. Your employer may add to your account, in some cases by matching a certain percentage of your contributions. The traditional 401(k) is the most common and well known defined contribution plan.

Regarding the individual retirement savings plans, the options are the traditional Individual Retirement Account (IRA) and the Roth IRA. The traditional IRA allows tax-deductible contributions while the Roth IRAs are not tax-deductible. However, the contributions to a Roth IRA can be withdrawn at any time without being subject to a penalty. Interest earned on the account, however, is subject to a penalty or tax.

With regards to how to fund your 401(k) and your IRA, you are going to have to take some time to study the various options and educate yourself. The choice will be easier with the 401(k) as your employer probably has a limited number of mutual funds to choose from. My advice is that you keep it simple and stick with index mutual funds, which offer the advantage of low fees and/or lifecycle funds, which are also low-cost and are automatically reweighted as you approach your retirement date.

During the course of building and managing your savings and investment portfolio, you are likely to consider using the services of a professional financial advisor at some point. Financial advisors generally fall into one of three categories: money managers, product salespeople, and financial planners. Money managers attempt to grow their portfolio, funds from numerous investors, and invest in some sector of the market in which they believe they have particular expertise that will allow them to generate higher rates of return than individuals can attain own their own. Of course their clients are expected to pay a premium for that expertise. Product salespeople typically place their own agenda, or that of their company, ahead of their client's. Their focus is often on selling clients a narrow range of products that come with high fees. I recommend you avoid this type of advisor.

The financial planner is an individual that takes a holistic view of their client's debts, their finances, considers their goals, and helps them develop a viable retirement plan to meet those goals while considering tax saving and various investment strategies. Should you decide you require, or desire, the services of a professional, your best bet is probably a financial planner. If considering a financial planner, seek one that is comfortable answering your questions, has a reasonable amount of experience, has attained some sort of certification, and whose fee is based on a flat hourly rate vice a percentage of your portfolio value.

An important philosophy to adopt is that of paying yourself first. Prior to paying your bills or spending money on entertainment, you should pay yourself. This is made easier as your 401(k) will be automatically deducted from your paychecks. Additionally, any technologically adept company you establish your IRA with should have an option for automatic withdrawals from your checking account; provide the option for making self-directed contributions, and the ability to transfer money between accounts; both inter-institution (e.g. your bank checking account to your IRA account) and intra-institution (e.g. your brokerage account to your IRA account). I strongly encourage you to take advantage of this capability. You will find that if you never see the money, you will not miss it.

[5] TRACK INVESTMENTS

A few years ago I created, and have subsequently modified a number of times, a spreadsheet for tracking and managing my retirement goals. The purpose was straight forward. I wanted one document that I could turn to which allowed me to identify my desired annual income in retirement, note the value of my present sources of passive income, record the projected value of my future sources of passive income, and determine the amount of money I need to invest on a monthly basis to reach my stated financial retirement goals. The factors that determine the amount of money that needs to be invested include the number of years until retirement, the present value of accounts, the anticipated rate of return, and current principal.

That spreadsheet, until recently void of a definitive name, is now titled the RWR Retirement Planner and has proven to be a very useful tool. It allows me to track where I am, relative to where I want to be, at any given time with regards to the value of my nest-egg. By conducting quarterly reviews, I can quickly assess if my investment strategy is producing the desired results. If not, I can use the planner to adjust key investment inputs (e.g. years to invest, rate of return, and annual contributions) to determine where changes to my plan can be made to stay on track.

Utilizing the RWR Retirement Planner

Some notes on utilizing the planner. The entries are marked with either blue or green pointers; information should be input - or viewed - in numerical sequence. When you receive your planner, you will note that entries marked with light blue pointers require user input or are adjustable by the user. Conversely, the green pointers are fixed formulas that adjust based on the various user inputs and are not user accessible. ***Note:*** *Cells such as 401(k): Spouse #1, under Portfolio Balances, and Social Security: Spouse #2, under Annual Passive Income, are unlocked which will allow you to personalize the entries as desired.*

Returning to our favorite family, the Smiths, to use an example, we see that they have increased their Desired Annual Retirement Income to $65,000 while their Current Principal remains at $17,500 (**Figure 12**).

Desired Annual Retirement Income	$65,000.00	1
Accounts		
401(k): Husband	$12,000.00	
401(k): Wife	$5,500.00	
IRA: Husband	$0.00	
IRA: Wife	$0.00	2
Brokerage Account	$0.00	
Miscellaneous Account	$0.00	
Miscellaneous Account	$0.00	
Checking Account	$0.00	
Cash	$0.00	
Current Principal	$17,500.00	3

Figure 12. Desired Annual Retirement Income

We also see that they do not have any sources of Present Passive Income and that they are currently assuming $56,000 in Future Passive Income from their current respective employers and Social Security (they opened SSA Accounts to view their projected benefits). The result is that they will be $9,000 short annually of their goal. Utilizing the 4% rule we previously discussed, we see that they will need a $225,000 nest-egg to meet that goal (**Figure 13**).

Annual Passive Income		
Present		
Pension: Husband	$0.00	4
Pension: Wife	$0.00	
Future		
Pension: Husband	$16,500.00	
Pension: Wife	$12,000.00	5
Social Security Pension: Husband	$15,000.00	
Social Security Pension: Wife	$12,500.00	
Secured Income	$56,000.00	6
Shortfall	$9,000.00	7
Investments Objective Utilizing the 4% Rule	$225,000.00	8

Figure 13. Annual Passive Income

The next task (**Figure 14**) for the Smiths is to observe their current principal (pointer 9, retrieved from pointer 3 cell), input the anticipated number of years until retirement (pointer 10), input the expected annual return rate (Pointer 11), input their current annual contributions (pointer 12), observe the monthly contributions that would have to be made (pointer 13) and then observe the Summary of Results (**Figure 15**).

The objective is to make adjustments to your Investment Inputs (Years to Retirement, Expected Annual Return Rate, and Annual Contributions - pointers 10, 11, and 12 respectively) until the Value After *x* Years (pointer 14, Summary of Results) meets or exceeds your investments objective utilizing the 4% Rule (pointer 8). And of course, as you increase your portfolio balances (pointer 2), you will be in a position to make favorable adjustments (e.g. reduce Years to Retirement, pointer 10).

Investment Inputs		
Current Principal	$17,500.00	9
Years to Retirement	15	10
Expected Annual Return Rate	5.50%	11
Annual Contributions	$7,070.00	12
Average Monthly Contributions	$589.17	13

Figure 14. Investment Inputs

Summary of Results		
Value After 15 Years	$206,211.20	14

Figure 15. Summary of Results

The Inflation Impact

Simply put, inflation reduces the value of your dollars, and the reduction in the value of your dollars will negatively impact your purchasing power. Unfortunately, inflation is one of those factors that cannot be controlled. This is one of those areas in planning your retirement that you will need to incorporate some art. While you can easily find historical information on the rate of inflation over any given time period - 1 year, 5 years, 10 years, etc. - and make a good estimate, the reality is it is just that, an estimate. As with most calculations, you are better off thinking more conservatively. In this case that means assume a higher rate of inflation vice a lower rate.

The four areas (Desired Annual Retirement Income, Annual Passive Income, Investment Inputs, and the Summary of Results) of the RWR Retirement Planner do not account for inflation. However, a separate Inflation Calculator is included on the spreadsheet as inflation is a factor you must be aware of as you plan and manage your savings and investments; and develop your retirement goals. One way to determine inflation's negative impact is to determine the value of today's dollar in the future. As an example, assume you have $5,000 today. Looking ahead 10 years - at a 1.5% annual rate of inflation - the value of that $5,000 would be reduced (referred to as Reduced Amount in the calculator) to $4,308.34. While you would still have $5,000, it would only be able to purchase $4,308.34 of the services and goods that you had purchased 10 years ago. Looking at it in a slightly different way, standing in the future looking back, if you wanted to be able to purchase all of the goods and services you purchased 10 years ago, you would now need (referred to as Required Amount in the Calculator) $5,802.70. As you develop your retirement goals and review your numbers, you must factor in the negative impacts of inflation.

One solution is to make an adjustment to your Desired Annual Retirement Income (pointer 1) on the RWR Retirement Planner. In our previous example with the Smith family, their desired income when they retire in 15 years is $65,000. Plugging those two numbers into the Inflation Calculator - along with their projected annual inflation rate of 1.5%, we see that the future value of $65,000 in today's dollars is $51,990.35. If they want the full purchasing power of $65,000 in the future, they will need $81,265.08 (**Figure 16**). In this scenario, the Smiths might adjust their Desired Annual Retirement Income to $81,265.08 and re-compute the other inputs in the RWR Retirement Planner.

Inflation Calculator	
Present Value	$65,000.00
Projected Annual Inflation Rate	1.50%
Number of Years	15
Required Amount	$81,265.08
Reduced Amount	$51,990.35

Figure 16. Inflation Calculator

Periodic Reviews

After you have opened your retirement savings accounts, establishing the framework for your investment portfolio, your work is not done. In fact, it will never really end. On a quarterly basis you should ask yourself the following questions. Has my situation (e.g. married or divorced, new job, promotion, etc.) changed? Have my goals (e.g. increase in desired annual retirement income) changed? Has the investment performance (e.g. a prolonged period where the rate of return was lower than expected) affected my goals? How much will I need to reach the new goals? Has the economic environment (e.g. legislative changes to Social Security or IRA rules) changed?

If you have adopted a more active investment strategy – utilizing a combination of individual stocks, bonds, and cash in your retirement savings – the answers to those questions will be particularly important as you may need to consider rebalancing your portfolio. However, even if you have adopted a more passive buy and hold strategy and your 401(k) and IRA accounts are comprised primarily of low activity index mutual funds and lifecycle funds, a quarterly review should be conducted. A buy and hold strategy does not mean buy and forget.

Your RWR Spending Planner and RWR Retirement Planner worksheets can serve as useful tools in tracking your expenses, answering the aforementioned questions, and tracking the value of your investments, ensuring that you are meeting your financial objectives or are in a position to increase contributions and aim a little higher. While you certainly do not want to obsess on these questions and make adjustments on a daily or weekly basis, you do want to review at regular intervals and make adjustments as necessary.

Chapter Summary

After you have conducted the initial review of your spending plan, made adjustments, opened your retirement savings accounts, and started funding those accounts, your work is not done. Your next step is to track and manage your investments, making sure you remain fiscally fit. The RWR Retirement Planner is a great tool for that purpose. The planner allows you to identify your desired annual income in retirement, note the value of present sources of passive income, record the projected value of future sources of passive income, and determine the amount of money needed to invest on a monthly basis to reach your stated retirement goals.

When utilizing the planner, remember that the entries are marked with either blue or green pointers and that information should be input - or viewed - in numerical sequence. The entries marked with light blue pointers require user input or are adjustable by the user. Conversely, the green pointers are fixed formulas that adjust based on the various user inputs and are not user accessible. As a means of personalization, some cells (e.g. 401(k): Spouse #1, under Portfolio Balances) remain unlocked.

When using the planner, ensure you give consideration to the impact of inflation. As the impact is difficult to know from year to year - this is one of those areas that lend credence to the idea that investing is as much art as science - you need to incorporate that element into your plan. A separate Inflation Calculator, which helps with the development and understanding of Required Amounts and Reduced Amounts, is included on the spreadsheet.

On a quarterly basis you should ask yourself questions regarding changes to your personal situation (e.g. divorce or marriage), goals (e.g. desire to retire sooner), the economic environment (e.g. change to IRA rules), and investment performance (e.g. better [worse] than expected) to determine if and how adjustment should be made to your retirement plan. This is particularly true if you have adopted a more active investment strategy – utilizing a combination of individual stocks, bonds, and cash in your retirement savings – vice a more passive buy and hold strategy and your 401(k) and IRA accounts are comprised primarily of low activity index mutual funds and lifecycle funds. You certainly do not want to obsess on these questions and make adjustments on a daily or weekly basis. However, you should review your RWR Retirement Planner at regular intervals and adjust as necessary.

[6] DRAWING DOWN YOUR NEST-EGG

Rate of Withdrawal

Accumulating and managing your money in the preceding years was one phase of a multi-phase effort. It was simply one part of the plan. Drawing down your nest-egg at the appropriate rate is an essential element of your retirement plan. It would be terrible if you spent a number of years building your nest-egg only to jeopardize your retirement by drawing it down too fast. Enter the 4% rule. As touched on previously, the rule was developed by William Bengen, A Southern California financial planner in the mid-1990s, as a tool for financial advisers in helping clients construct their retirement plans.

Basically the rule says that if you take out 4% of your nest-egg the first year in retirement, and then adjust that rate to account for inflation in each subsequent year (e.g. if inflation rises 1% during your first year of retirement, you would withdraw 5% of your nest-egg during your second year in retirement), you will not run out of money for at least three decades. This idea is based on the oft-stated historical returns for an investor with a portfolio comprised of 60% large company stocks and 40% bonds. While there is some doubt about the veracity of the rule - some believe it is simply too arbitrary, some believe it is too high, and some believe too low - it provides a good starting point.

As a means of comparison, you can search the Internet and find tables that will show how long assets will last at rates other than 4% (1 – 7% are typically shown) and a combination of other factors such as different time periods, generally ranging from 20 – 30 years, and different mixtures of stocks/bonds. Again however, whatever shortcomings it may have, the 4% rule serves as a good starting point for most individuals as they develop their retirement plans. In addition to variations of the 4% rule, there are alternatives, including the interest only strategy and a relatively new approach, using the IRS' Required Minimum Distribution (RMD) guidelines as a withdrawal strategy; and I would be remiss if I did not point them out.

The interest only strategy dictates that retirees leave the principal in their retirement accounts untouched and spend only the dividends on stocks and the interest on bonds or certificates of deposit. While this strategy can work for wealthy individuals, it has serious drawbacks for most retirees (Sun &Webb, 2012). As examples, 5% interest earned in one year on a modest retirement nest-egg of $200,000 provides only $10,000 annually or $833.33 each month; and 6% on a $300,000 nest-egg is only $18,000 annually or $1,500 each month. Neither amount is likely to sustain you in retirement.

The RMD strategy basically utilizes the withdrawal rates imposed by the IRS for minimum distributions from IRAs and defined contribution plans once account holders reach the age of 70½. For a closer look at these strategies and more detail, particularly the RMD strategy, please refer to *Can Retirees Base Wealth Withdrawals on the IRS' Required Minimum Distributions?* The brief, prepared by the Center for Retirement Research at Boston College, does a nice job of comparing the different strategies and pointing out some pros and cons. Also, you can simply search the Internet for *RMD as the rate of withdrawal* for a take on the strategy from a number of other sources.

Order of Withdrawal

As we have touched on previously, the RMD is a condition imposed on retirement accounts by the IRS. The RMD is the amount the IRS mandates the owner of an individual retirement account must withdraw each year. Traditional IRAs, SEP and SIMPLE accounts, as well as employer sponsored retirement plans, such as 401(k) plans are subject to RMD. The RMD minimum IRA distribution begins once the qualified account owner reaches age 70½. At that age, IRA withdrawals are required to begin no later than April 1 of the following year.

One caveat, if you are still working at 70½ and still contributing to a defined contribution plan such as a 401(k) or 403(b), you are can postpone your RMD. Provided that you do not own more than five percent of a company and your retirement plan permits it, you can delay the RMDs until April 1 after the year that you leave the service of that company. Keep in mind however, that the delay only applies to the 401(k) plan of the company for which you are still working. If you have other 401(k) benefits from previous employers, you will still be required to take your RMD from those accounts at 70½. Your best course of action is to research the latest information and your options on the IRA website, or discuss with a financial planner if you find yourself in this situation as you approach 70 years of age.

It is often stated that Roth IRAs are not subject to Required Minimum Distributions. That is not completely accurate. While Roth IRAs are not subject to Required Minimum Distributions during the owner's lifetime (the most valuable attribute of the Roth IRA to many), they are subject to RMD after the owner's death. See **Table 1** for specific guidance and comparison between different retirement accounts.

Table 1. RMD Comparison Chart

Required Minimum Distributions for Account Owners		
	IRAs including SEP, SIMPLE and SARSEP IRAs	**Defined Contribution Plans**
When do I take my first RMD (the required beginning date)?	You must take your first RMD by April 1 of the year following the year in which you turn 70½, regardless of whether you are still employed.	April 1 of the year following the later of the year you turn 70 ½ or the year you retire (if allowed by your plan). If you are a 5% owner, you must start RMDs by April 1 of the year following the year you turn 70½.
When do I reach age 70½?	You reach age 70½ on the date that is 6 calendar months after the date of your 70th birthday. **Example**: Your 70th birthday was June 30, 2010. You reached age 70½ on December 30, 2010. You must take your first RMD (for 2010) by April 1, 2011. **Example**: Your 70th birthday was July 1, 2010. You reached age 70½ on January 1, 2011. You do not have an RMD for 2010. You must take your first RMD (for 2011) by April 1, 2012.	Same as IRA rule
What is the deadline for taking subsequent RMDs after the first RMD?	After the first RMD, you must take subsequent RMDs by December 31 of each year beginning with the calendar year containing your required beginning date. **Example**: You turn 70½ on July 15, 2010. You must take your first RMD, for 2010, by April 1, 2011. You must take your second RMD, for 2011, by December 31, 2011, and your third RMD, for	Same as IRA rule

	2012, by December 31, 2012.	
How do I calculate my RMD?	Your RMD is generally determined by dividing the adjusted market value of your IRAs as of December 31 of the preceding year by the distribution period that corresponds with your age in the Uniform Lifetime Table (Table III in IRS Publication 590, ***Individual Retirement Arrangements (IRAs)***). If your spouse is your sole beneficiary and is more than 10 years younger than you, you will use the Joint Life and Last Survivor Expectancy Table (Table II in IRS Publication 590). Required Minimum Distribution Worksheets	Same as IRA rule Your plan sponsor/administrator should calculate the RMD for you.
How should I take my RMDs if I have multiple accounts?	If you have more than one IRA, you must calculate the RMD for each IRA separately each year. However, you may aggregate your RMD amounts for all of your IRAs and withdraw the total from one IRA or a portion from each of your IRAs. You do not have to take a separate RMD from each IRA.	If you have more than one defined contribution plan, you must calculate and satisfy your RMDs separately for each plan and withdraw that amount from that plan. Exception: If you have more than one 403(b) tax-sheltered annuity account, you can total the RMDs and then take them from any one (or more) of the tax-sheltered annuities.
May I withdraw more than the RMD?	Yes, an IRA owner can always withdraw more than the RMD. You cannot apply excess withdrawals toward future years' RMDs.	Same as IRA rule
May I take more than one withdrawal in a	You may withdraw your annual RMD in any number of distributions throughout the	Same as IRA rule

year to meet my RMD?	year, as long as you withdraw the total annual minimum amount by December 31 (or April 1 if it is for your first RMD).	
What happens if I do not take the RMD?	If the distributions to you in any year are less than the RMD for that year, you are subject to an additional tax equal to 50% of the undistributed RMD.	Same as IRA rule

Note*: There are no RMD requirements for a Roth IRA while the owner is alive. However, designated Roth accounts are subject to the RMD rules.*

Source: Internal Revenue Service (2013)

As discussed previously, most families preparing for retirement will have a combination of tax-deferred (e.g. traditional IRAs and 401[k]s), taxable (i.e. any cash or personal account where you can purchase investments), and tax exempt (e.g. Roth IRAs) accounts. By withdrawing money from the various accounts in the most advantageous sequence, you will improve the portfolio's tax efficiency and increase its longevity.

If you are 70½ years of age, the general rule of thumb is to first withdraw from accounts where RMDs are mandated. However, if you have maintained a good level of fiscal fitness, it is likely that you are retired long before 70½ years of age. For most retirees, the order of withdrawal - before they reach 70½ years of age and are dealing with the withdrawals mandated by RMD - will be from taxable accounts, then tax-deferred accounts, and then tax exempt accounts.

Taxable accounts are withdrawn first as they are generally taxed at favorable dividend and capital gains rates and only on the capital appreciation, not the entire withdrawal amount. With tax-deferred accounts, you will pay a higher tax rate on a greater amount of income. If you withdraw from tax-deferred accounts sooner, vice later, you will accelerate income taxes and reduce the tax-deferred growth. Once the taxable portfolio has been depleted, look to tax-advantaged accounts where the determination to spend from tax-deferred or tax exempt investments depends primarily on current - vice future - tax rate assumptions. If you expect future tax rates will be higher than current rates, it generally makes sense to withdraw from tax-deferred accounts first. Conversely, if you anticipate your future tax rate will be lower than your current one, you should spend from tax exempt accounts first.

Unfortunately, there is not one clear cut answer to how to go about withdrawing money from your various retirement accounts and the options will vary depending on your unique situation. As you approach your desired retirement date, perhaps four to five years in advance, you will need to assess how much money you have in each respective account, what are the tax implications for withdrawals, determine if there are required distributions, and what the various options are for withdrawal from each respective account. As an example, the TSP provides options for partial withdrawals and full withdrawals (which includes sub-options such as a single payment, a series of monthly payments, an annuity, and a mixed withdrawal) and of course, each has various rules and considerations.

Making developing a withdrawal plan even more challenging is that you must consider each of your sources of retirement income (IRAs, 401(k)s, defined benefit plans, Social Security, etc.) not only on their own, but in the context of where they fit into your overall retirement portfolio, to determine the most advantageous strategy. While it might seem a bit overwhelming, it is much better to be in a position trying to determine how to withdraw money from multiple sources vice not having any, or only one source, of retirement income.

Reflecting back on our discussion about financial advisors, this is a point in your retirement planning where a good advisor can be very beneficial as there are a number of factors that must be considered as you settle on a withdrawal plan. Sometimes there is great value in getting a second opinion, one that can be a little more objective, and can help identify impacts you may have overlooked. As I noted previously, like a good friend of mine that recently started consulting with a professional advisor, I plan to do the same thing when I get within four or five years of retirement.

Relocating in Retirement

While most retirees will choose to stay in their current location following retirement, the change in life status might be a good time to consider the possibility of relocating. Retirement might offer the chance to live in a home that costs less to maintain, live in a community with better public transportation, live in an area with a more favorable climate, the chance to be closer to children/grandchildren, live in a city with access to better dental and health care, or within a community that offers superior local amenities.

There are a number of websites with various tools that help with comparing retirement factors; and briefs that report the results of questionnaires and studies, which can assist in comparing different communities. One excellent source is the U.S. Census Bureau (U.S. Department of Commerce) website that offers tools such as State & County QuickFacts and the American Community Survey. The QuickFacts provide statistics for all states and counties, and for cities and towns with populations that exceed 5,000 people. QuickFacts allows visitors to view information such as population, education rates, home ownership rates, per capita income, and persons per square mile.

The American Community Survey (ACS) is a nationwide survey which provides more detailed demographic, social, economic, housing, and financial data on an annual basis. Demographic characteristics include factors such as age and sex; social characteristics include factors such as marital status and ancestry; economic characteristics include items such as income and health insurance coverage; housing characteristics touch on residence types, home ages, and plumbing/heating facts; and financial characteristics include owner/renter tenures, housing values, rent costs, and selected monthly owner costs. While these types of information are often considerations for those approaching retirement, it is typical for respondents to mention cost of living as the most significant factor in their decision to relocate, or to consider relocation, in many retirement surveys. A significant factor affecting cost of living? Taxes.

While planning retirement, many people pay close attention to how a particular state treats state income tax. However, there are a number of other taxes that should be considered if relocating is a thought for you: state sales tax, fuel tax, personal Income tax, taxes on retired military pay, retirement Income taxes, and property taxes to name a few. In addition to taxes, other cost of living factors to consider include food, housing, utilities, transportation, and health care. There are a number of online calculators to help with comparing the cost of living in different areas. If you are considering relocation following retirement, I recommend that you leverage the Internet to research potential retirement locations, their cost of living, your potential tax liabilities, and factors such as demographics and social characteristics.

Chapter Summary

Once you have built the nest-egg that will allow you to retire comfortably and are preparing for your transition into retirement, you will need to develop a withdrawal plan. Accumulating and managing your money in the preceding years was simply one phase of a multi-phase effort. The first thing to consider is the rate of withdrawal from your retirement account. The most well known strategy is the "4% Rule" which was developed in the mid-1990s by William Bengen, A Southern California financial planner. While not universally praised as a strategy, it serves as a useful starting point to determine the rate of withdrawal for most people.

As might be expected, there are alternative strategies to the 4% rule including the interest only strategy and a relatively new approach, using the IRS' Required Minimum Distribution (RMD) guidelines as a withdrawal strategy. While the interest only strategy is only practical for a small group of retirees, the IRS' RMD as a withdrawal strategy is a more practical, potential approach for many retirees. Whichever approach is taken, remember there are no guarantees as some elements of retirement planning are as much art as science.

Just as the IRS imposes rules governing contributions, they also impose rules mandating withdrawals, manifested in the RMD. It is the amount the IRS requires the owner of an individual retirement account to withdrawal each year. Traditional IRAs, SEP and SIMPLE accounts, as well as employer sponsored retirement plans, such as 401(k) plans are subject to RMD. The RMD minimum IRA distribution begins once the qualified account owner reaches age 70½. Upon reaching age 70 ½, IRA withdrawals must begin no later than April 1 of the following year.

Once you reach 70 ½ years of age, the general rule of thumb is to first withdraw from accounts where RMDs are mandated. However, if you have maintained a good level of fiscal fitness, it is likely that you are retired long before 70½ years of age. Therefore, you must consider the order of withdrawals from your retirement accounts before that time. For most retirees, it is reasonable to start with the assumption that the order of withdrawal should be from taxable accounts, then tax-deferred accounts, and then finally from tax exempt accounts.

Unfortunately, there is not one clear cut answer to how to go about withdrawing money from your various retirement accounts and the options will vary depending on your unique situation. As you approach your desired retirement date, perhaps four to five years in advance, you will need to assess how much money you have in each respective account, what are the tax implications for withdrawals, determine if there are required distributions, and what the various options are for withdrawal from each respective account. Making developing a withdrawal plan even more challenging is that you must consider each of your sources of retirement income (IRAs, 401(k)s, defined benefit plans, Social Security, etc.) not only within the context of their own rules, but in combination with your other accounts to determine the most advantageous strategy. This is potentially a point in executing your retirement plan when utilizing a financial planner probably makes good sense.

And finally, while most retirees will choose to stay in their current location, retirement might be a good time to consider the possibility of relocating. Retirement might offer the chance to live in a home that costs less to maintain, live in a community that offers superior local amenities, reside in an area with a more favorable climate, or the chance to be closer to children/grandchildren. There are a number of online calculators to help with comparing the cost of living in different areas. I recommend that you leverage the Internet to research potential retirement locations, their cost of living, and your potential tax liabilities if you believe relocating is a potential option for you.

[7] PHILOSOPHIES AND RANDOM THOUGHTS

Defining Wealth

As you conduct more research, read more material, and become more enlightened with regards to personal finance and retirement, you will stumble across many different definitions of wealth and begin to form your own opinion. While some consider investable assets ($500,000, $1,000,000?), some think in terms of income ($100,000, $150,000 or $400,000 per year?), while others might consider some combination of investable assets and income, while also mixing in consideration of a home's value when forming their definition. While there is not necessarily a right or wrong definition, none of those strike me as providing deep insight into how a given figure translates into providing a quality of life, or a desired lifestyle, in retirement for an individual or their family. The definition I settled on years ago, shaped in part by Mr. Gibbon's quote, involves the understanding of expenses and their relationship to the three types of income: earned income, portfolio income, and passive income.

Earned income as defined by the IRS is all the taxable income and wages you get from working or from certain disability payments. For most people it is simply the money earned at a job while working for someone else. This is the type of income most are familiar with and the only source of income for many families. It is generally considered the least desirable type of income for that very reason. You are completely dependent on someone else for your livelihood and have less control.

Portfolio income is the interest, dividends, and any other forms of payment received on the investments within your portfolio. Additionally, portfolio income also includes capital gains, realized from trading instruments such as ETFs, stocks, bonds, mutual funds, currencies, commodities, etc. For most people, investing in the stock market is the most common form of building wealth and portfolio income.

And finally, passive income is the money you get from activities you performed in the past but are no longer required to do for an income or income from activities you no longer participate in (e.g. a pension from a previous job); the creation and selling of intellectual property (e.g. books, patents, or music); or assets that you have purchased (e.g. renting a house, assuming the amount collected in rent exceeds the mortgage payment) from which you receive income. The key difference between earned income and the latter two is that you have greater control.

With those descriptions of the three types of income as the backdrop, the definition of wealth that I have adopted is, "*you are wealthy when you and your family can live your chosen lifestyle on portfolio and passive income; and no longer require earned income.*" While you may still choose to work at that point, it is just that, a choice. Ultimately, wealth and a comfortable retirement are not about a specific income level, a specific portfolio balance, or a specific dollar amount; it is about managing your portfolio is such a way that you have a wide variety of choices regarding when you retire, where you retire, and how you spend your time in retirement. Indeed, it is about getting to a point where your passive and portfolio income is superior to your expenses and your wishes can be met.

Do Not Loan Money

At first glance, that statement might strike many as quite miserly. Nothing could be further from the truth. I am not suggesting that you should never help friends and family in the form of monetary assistance. I am simply saying that you should consider it a gift vice a loan. A loan implies that the money should be repaid at some point in the future. There are two reasons why I believe this is a practice better avoided. First, money has a tendency to put a strain on relationships, particularly if the recipient has a difficult time repaying the loan or is late with repayment. They are stressed because of their desire to repay the loan, and the lender is stressed because they had expectations of repayment, and likely, a plan for using the loaned funds for some other purpose. Second, the practice can be disruptive to your retirement planning.

As we touched on previously, once you establish your retirement plan and have identified the amount you need to invest on a monthly basis to meet your goals, your first priority should be to pay yourself first. If a situation arises and you have determined that a family or friend has a sincere need for financial assistance, and providing that assistance will not impact your plan, you should assist with a gift vice a loan. I assure you that if you loan a family member $300 of the $500 you were going to commit to your Roth IRA one particular month and they are not able to repay you, they are going to feel bad, you are going to feel resentment, and you will be $300 – not even counting the compound interest you will not have earned – further from your objective. Conversely, if you find that you have an additional $150 at your disposal after meeting your monthly financial goals, and you can assist a family member with a gift of half the $300 they may need, they will be very appreciative, you will be glad you could assist, and there is no chance for resentment and strain on the relationship. Once you write that check for $150 it is forgotten forever and you move on and prepare to meet your next month's goal.

Do Not Raid Retirement Accounts

Once the balances in your retirement accounts start to grow and you get well positioned on your rendezvous with retirement, there will probably be an occasion (e.g. helping a child with college tuition) when you will be tempted to borrow against your nest-egg. Generally speaking, you should not. Like the previous philosophy, I know this sounds a little miserly, particularly if we are talking about assisting a child with college costs. However, there are numerous reasons why you should not tap into your retirement accounts. Consider the money in your 401(k). First, any money that you withdraw is no longer in its tax-protected status, doing what it does best, leveraging the power of compound interest. Second, over the long-term, you are significantly less likely to make more money by lending funds to yourself, or your child (e.g. for college), than you would have made had you left the money invested in your 401(k) account.

A third consideration, what happens if you borrow money from your 401(k) and then lose or quit your job? Answer, it is likely that you will be required to pay back the entire loan within a short time period. If you cannot pay back the loan within the given time period, you will be subjected to a 10% penalty on the balance of the funds if you are under 59½ years of age. Additionally, you will have to pay income taxes on the money because even though you might consider it a loan, the IRS will consider it an early withdrawal. If you, or a child, require a loan, you are better off seeking a more traditional loan vice dipping into your 401(k).

View Your House as a Home, Not an Asset

While there isn't necessarily a great debate raging, there are strong opinions on both sides of the question, *"is a home an asset or a liability?"* There are those that believe the home they live in should be considered an asset. However, there is a school of thought, popularized by Robert Kiyosaki (author of *Rich Dad Poor Dad*), that says a home, particularly one carrying a mortgage, is a liability. Before we go any further, let's look at Merriam-Webster's definition of these two key words:

as·set [ˈa-ˌset also -sət] *noun*

- A valuable person or thing
- Something that is owned by a person, company, etc.

li·a·bil·i·ty [ˌlī-ə-ˈbi-lə-tē] *noun*

- The state of being legally responsible for something
- The state of being liable for something
- Something (such as the payment of money) for which a person or business is legally responsible

Looking at those two definitions, a case could be made for both. There is no doubt that many have sold their home at a great profit, supporting the idea that a house can be a valuable thing, an asset. On the other hand, when your home is carrying a mortgage, you are liable for the home and you are legally responsible for making payments. That would clearly make it a liability. Something to consider when you look at housing as a whole. From 1890 through 2012, on average, home prices gained absolutely nothing in value after adjusting for inflation.

What does it all mean? You are better off viewing your primary residence as a liability and not as an investment. When considering preparation for retirement, it is better to look strictly at portfolio value (aka financial wealth) – which excludes things like home and car values – which are traditionally included in net worth, which is determined by subtracting the total dollar amount of all liabilities from the total value of all assets. The rationale? When you are ready to retire, who cares how much Kelly Blue Book believes your car is worth or how much Zillow believes your house is worth? Those numbers are largely irrelevant.

While having a significant net worth may sound impressive, it isn't particularly helpful if the majority of that number is based on what you – or Zillow – believe your house is worth. In the 2007 time frame, prior to home prices crashing, there were a lot of people with inflated beliefs regarding their net worth, which was largely based on perceived home values. There are lots of people out there that profit from selling the idea that a home is a valuable asset and you should do everything in your power to own one. That is not always the case and you shouldn't.

Even if you do everything right (e.g. buy the right sized house, buy at a good price, get a fixed rate loan, etc.), you will be better served by viewing your home as a liability and not give it consideration when calculating your net worth (or at least understand the difference between net worth and financial wealth) and conducting retirement planning. If you are interested in investing in real estate, consider purchasing a rental property or Real Estate Investment Trusts (REITs). With respect to retirement, and specifically generating retirement income, it is much more useful to focus on passive and portfolio income, not your home.

Know What You Can Afford

How many times have you gone out to purchase a big ticket item (i.e. house, car, or major appliance) and after the sales person checked your credit report, you were told what you can afford? Think about that. The salesperson is telling you what you what you can afford. Unless that person has access to your RWR Spending Plan Worksheet as well as your RWR Retirement Planner, they cannot possibly know where you are with regards to meeting your retirement savings and investment objectives; and what you can afford. At this point, hopefully you know the difference between what someone is willing to loan you (and what they think you can afford) and what you know you can afford based on your thoughtfully constructed retirement plan. Prior to getting anywhere close to a car dealership or your local big box retailer, you should have already consulted your retirement tools, run your numbers, and know exactly what you are willing to pay and what you are able to afford in order to remain fiscally fit and stay on track with your retirement plan.

Disregard the Naysayers

Regardless of the endeavor you are undertaking, no matter what it is that you might be trying to accomplish, there are likely to be those that tell you that you cannot achieve, you will not achieve, or you should not pursue your goal. You are likely to encounter these naysayers at some point on your road to fiscal fitness. I do not believe that the intent of most of the naysayers is malicious. In most cases I believe it is simply a lack of vision, an inability to see beyond the walls they have established for themselves. If they cannot imagine something for themselves, they certainly cannot imagine it for someone else.

When I first began my journey on the road to fiscal fitness, I would often mention the desired size of my nest-egg in conversations with others or the amount I was saving and investing on a monthly basis. While the amount changed periodically as I adjusted my aim upwards, the feedback was often the same. Negative. Generally the pessimism revolved around a couple of ideas. First, there was the belief that there was no way that I could save the amount of money required to get to the desired amount. And second, why would I sacrifice so much today for some future goal? The two things that I always keep in mind are that my goals are my own and there is nothing to stop me from taking the actions my plan dictates that I take; especially someone else's belief of what is possible.

Although you are bound to encounter naysayers, I still encourage you to engage in conversations on the topic of retirement savings. Just as I am certain you will receive some negative feedback, I am just as certain there will be the occasional conversation, or part of a conversation, that will yield a valuable nugget of information; something useful that can be used to enhance your fiscal fitness and improve your retirement prospects.

Find Your Balance and Courage

I am certain that you already know that there is no simple answer to the question of, *"how do you find the proper balance between living for today and preparing for tomorrow?"* As with most other endeavors and facets of your life, too much focus on one element, such as living all out today, at the exclusion of another, such as saving for tomorrow, will likely yield terrible results. Similarly, you do not want to only focus on preparing for tomorrow at the exclusion of enjoying life today. For me, development of the RWR Retirement Planner, and the adoption of various behaviors (e.g. paying myself first) and philosophies (e.g. knowing what I can afford) that work in conjunction with the planner, went a long way with helping me find my balance. By getting my debt under control and developing a spending plan, I was able to get control of my money. Once that control was established, I was able to utilize the power of the planner to determine what kind of annual income I could achieve, and that would sustain me and those I love, in retirement.

The practice of paying myself first (meeting the contribution goals as noted on my planner) and then paying my bills before spending money on extracurricular activities and entertainment has served me well. The truth is that I rarely feel as though I am sacrificing, or missing out on something, because I am saving and investing *x* number of dollars each month. Ironically, it seems as though I have more discretionary income now that I am focused on preparing for my retirement than I did prior to getting fit.

One note, discretionary income is typically defined as *"the amount of money that is available to a family for spending and saving after accounting for income taxes and personal necessities such as housing and food."* I like to give that definition a slight twist and opine that discretionary income is, *"the amount of money that is available to a family for spending after accounting for income taxes, saving/investing, and personal necessities such as housing and food."* A subtle difference to be sure, but one that is reflective of the attitudes and behaviors that I believe are necessary to meet retirement goals. As counterintuitive as it may seem, the more money you save and invest for tomorrow - within the structure of a solid plan - the more money you have to enjoy your life today.

A final thought with regards to finding your balance. One of the things I communicate to people when they express some apprehension or fear about taking the first step on what is bound to be a long journey, is that there will come a point where it is 5, 10, and 15 years in the future. Of that there is no doubt. Unless they are the victim of an unfortunate accident or illness, they will be a part of that future. The question is, *"where will they be in that future?"* Nothing worse than saying, *"if I would have done x, y, or z 10 years ago when I first started thinking of it, this is where I would be today."*

A quick story about my wife Karen is illustrative of this idea. As we approached marriage, I encouraged her to get her degree, something she had mentioned previously but not taken any concrete steps to pursue. I noted, and she agreed, that it would probably pay dividends in her professional life, and even if it did not, a lot of personal satisfaction would be gained. We agreed that the best course of action was to take one traditional brick and mortar class initially just to get her feet wet. Like a lot of schools today, the community college she started at offers traditional as well as online courses.

I remember when she came home from that first class doubting if she could make it as she had been out of school a number of years and was not sure she could handle the course work. Additionally, she noted that she believed she was the oldest person in the class. I encouraged her by noting that whether she went to school or not, time was going to pass. There was going to be a point when it was five years from that day and it was only a question of would she have a degree at that point or not. Five years later, in February 2011, my wife graduated with a Bachelors Degree in Business Administration, all while working full-time during her pursuit of the degree. Her story is not only a testament to her character, but of the fact that time will always pass; it is only a question of what you are doing as it is passing.

Do not be that person that says, *"If only I had done x years ago .... "* Do not have that regret. Find your balance and start doing today, not tomorrow or next Monday, what you know will pay significant dividends in your future. Best of luck!

GLOSSARY OF TERMS

NOTE: While all of the terms in this glossary were not touched upon in this book, you are likely to encounter many of these as you continue to educate yourself and prepare for retirement. Consider this Glossary of Terms your quick reference guide.

401(k): A qualified plan established by employers to which eligible employees may make salary deferral (salary reduction) contributions on a post-tax and/or pretax basis. Employers offering a 401(k) plan may make matching or non-elective contributions to the plan on behalf of eligible employees and may also add a profit-sharing feature to the plan. Earnings accrue on a tax-deferred basis. It is named after the section of the Internal Revenue Service Code that authorized the plan.

403(B): Named after the section of the Internal Revenue Service Code that authorized it, the plan is similar to a 401(k) but is available only to employees of hospitals, schools, churches, and certain other tax-exempt organizations. Employees may make salary deferral contributions that are usually limited by regulatory caps. Individual accounts in a 403(b) plan can be any of the following types: an annuity contract, which is provided through an insurance company; custodial account, which is invested in mutual funds; or a retirement income account set up for church employees.

Actively Managed Fund: Unlike an index fund, an actively managed fund has a fund manager or management team that picks stocks to buy and sell. Because of the active management strategy, these funds are usually more expensive than index funds.

Annual Percentage Yield (APY): The percentage on interest-bearing deposit accounts that reflect the total interest to be earned based on an institution's compounding method, assuming funds remain in the account for a 365-day year.

Annuity: A contract between you, the annuity owner, and an insurance company. In return for your lump sum payment - or series of payments - the insurance company agrees to provide either a regular stream of income or a lump sum pay-out at some future date.

Appreciation: The increase in the value of an investment over time.

Asset: A resource of monetary value, including cash, accounts receivable, inventory, real estate, machinery, collectibles, and securities.

Asset Allocation: The assignment of investment funds to broad categories of assets.

Balanced Fund: A mutual fund that maintains a balanced portfolio, generally around 50% stocks and 50% bonds, though the percentages can vary somewhat.

Broker: The individual or firm that conducts investment trades for you. The broker receives a commission or trading fee for their services.

Spending Plan (Budget): An itemized listing of current expenses. A spending plan allows an individual to carefully track how much money they are taking in during a given period, and figure out the best way to divide it among a variety of categories. Moreover, a spending plan provides an opportunity to see where changes can be made with regards to expenses; a reduction in one category necessarily means an opportunity for increasing in another and vice versa. By effectively managing a spending plan, an individual is less likely to overspend, and more likely to meet their financial goals.

Bureau of Labor Statistics: The Bureau of Labor Statistics of the U.S. Department of Labor is the principal Federal agency responsible for measuring labor market activity, working conditions, and price changes in the economy. Its mission is to collect, analyze, and disseminate essential economic information to support public and private decision-making.

Buy-and-Hold: A strategy in which the stock portion of an investor's portfolio is fully invested, including dividends reinvestments, at all times.

Capital Gain: An increase from the purchase price to the selling price of common stock or any other capital asset; profit from the sale of investments or property.

Capital Loss: A decrease from the purchase price to the selling price of common stock or any other capital asset; loss from the sale of investments or property.

Cash Equivalents: See *Money Market Instruments.*

Congressional Budget Office (CBO): The CBO produces

independent analyses of budgetary and economic issues to support the Congressional budget process. The agency is strictly nonpartisan and conducts objective, impartial analysis, which is evident in each of the dozens of reports and hundreds of cost estimates that its economists and policy analysts produce each year. All of CBO's products, apart from informal cost estimates for legislation being developed privately by Members of Congress or their staffs, are available to the Congress and the public on CBO's website.

Consumer Price Index (CPI): Tracked by the U.S. Department of Labor (Bureau of Labor Statistics), the CPI program produces monthly data on changes in the prices paid by urban consumers for a representative basket of goods and services.

Compound interest: Interest which is calculated not only on the initial principal but also the accumulated interest of prior periods.

Cost-of- Living Allowance (COLA): An increase to a wage, salary, or pension designed so that the real value remains the same; a cost-of-living adjustment increases the underlying wage, salary, or pension so that it keeps pace with inflation. Though federal pensions and Social Security include cost-of-living adjustments, many other pensions do not.

Credit Report: A report containing detailed information on an individual's credit history, including identifying information, bankruptcies, late payments, credit accounts, loans, and recent inquiries. An individual's report can be obtained the individual or by prospective lenders with the individual's permission, to determine his or her creditworthiness.

Deflation: The increase of purchasing power due to a general decrease in the prices of goods and services.

Depreciation: The decrease in the value of an investment over time.

Discretionary Income: The amount of money that is available to a family for spending after accounting for income taxes, saving/investing, and personal necessities such as housing and food.

Diversification: Dividing investment funds among a variety of securities with different risks and different rewards in an effort to minimize risk.

Dividend: A sum of money, determined by a company's directors, paid to shareholders of a corporation out of earnings.

Dollar Cost Averaging: A technique designed to reduce market risk through the systematic purchase of investment assets at predetermined intervals and set amounts. This practice lowers an investor's cost basis and reduces risk.

Dow Jones Industrial Average (DJIA): Price-weighted average of 30 actively traded blue-chip stocks, traditionally of industrial companies. Current Dow stocks include American Express® (AXP), Bank of America® (BAC), Cisco® (CSCO), Walt Disney ® (DIS), Microsoft ® (MSFT), and Wal-Mart® (WMT) to name a few.

Earned Income: Defined by the IRS as all the taxable income and wages you get from working or from certain disability payments. For most people it is the money earned at a job while working for someone else

.

Elective Contribution: This type of contribution is usually a deferral or percentage of a participant's salary. When an eligible employee decides to contribute a percentage of their paycheck to the 401(k) plan they are making an *'elective'* contribution.

Equity: An instrument that signifies an ownership position, or equity, in a corporation, and represents a claim on its proportionate share in the corporation's assets and profits.

Employee Stock ownership Plans (ESOPs): The employer pays a designated amount, often borrowed, into a fund which then is invested primarily in company stock. Any debt incurred in the purchase of the stock is repaid by the company. Stock then is distributed to employees according to a predetermined formula.

Exchange Trade Fund (ETF): A security that tracks an index, a commodity or a basket of assets like an index fund, but trades like a stock on an exchange. Unlike index funds, ETFs experience price changes throughout the day as they are bought and sold.

Expense Ratio: For a mutual fund, operating costs, including management fees, expressed as a percentage of the fund's average net assets for a given time period. The expense ratio does not include brokerage costs and various other transaction costs that may also contribute to a fund's total expenses.

Fee Structure: A chart or list showing the fees that an advisor or company charges for various services or activities. The structure lets customers or clients know what to expect when working with a particular advisor and their company.

Fiscal: Of or pertaining to finance or finances.

Full Retirement Age (FRA): Full retirement age is the age at which a person may first become entitled to full retirement benefits.

Investment: An asset or item that is purchased with the hope that it will generate income or appreciate in the future. In an economic sense, an investment is the purchase of goods that are not consumed today but are used in the future to create wealth. In finance, an investment is a monetary asset purchased with the idea that the asset will provide income in the future or appreciate and be sold at a higher price.

Investment Portfolio: An investor's collection of securities such as stocks, bonds, mutual funds, money market funds, and exchange traded funds.

Individual Retirement Account (IRA): Traditional IRAs are held by custodians, such as commercial banks and retail brokers, and investors can place IRA funds into stocks, bonds, mutual funds, ETFs, and other financial assets deemed fit by the custodian. When the individual begins receiving distributions from a traditional IRA, the income is treated as ordinary income and may be subjected to income tax. For individuals over the age of 50, higher annual contribution limits normally apply. Distributions are required to come out of the account by the time the account owner reaches 70½ years of age.

A Roth IRA bears many similarities to the traditional IRA, but contributions are not tax deductible and qualified distributions are tax free. Similar to other retirement plans, non-qualified distributions from a Roth IRA may be subject to a penalty upon withdrawal. A qualified distribution is one that is taken at least five years after the taxpayer establishes his or her first Roth IRA and when he or she is age 59 ½, disabled, using the withdrawal to purchase a first home (limit $10,000), or deceased (in which case the beneficiary collects). Qualified distributions from a Roth IRA are always tax free as taxes are paid in the year the contributions are made.

Lifecycle Fund: A mutual fund holding a portfolio of other mutual fund shares managed according to a specified target date. The fund moves toward a more conservative mix (a larger proportion of bonds and smaller proportion of stocks) as the target - retirement - date draws closer.

Market Risk: The chance that the value of an investment will decline to a level below its current market price.

Macroeconomics: The branch of economics that studies the behavior of the economy as a whole. It considers economics on a larger scale. This branch examines economy-wide phenomena such as changes in unemployment, national income, rate of growth, gross domestic product (GDP), and inflation.

Microeconomics: The branch of economics that examines the market behavior of individual consumers in an attempt to understand their behavior and decision-making process. It considers economics on a smaller scale as it focuses on the interaction between individual buyers and sellers and the factors that influence the choices they make. In particular, this branch focuses on patterns of supply and demand and the determination of price and output in individual markets.

Money Market Funds: Mutual funds whose investments are limited to money market instruments or other securities with average maturities that are usually measurable in days.

Money Market Instruments: Commercial paper, certificates of deposit, treasury bills, and other fixed income securities with maturities of less than one year. Also known as Cash Equivalents.

Mutual Fund: An investment vehicle that is made up of a group of funds collected from many investors for the purpose of investing in securities such as stocks, bonds, money market instruments and similar assets.

NASDAQ: An American stock exchange owned by NASDAQ OMX Group. It is the second largest stock market comparing to official stock exchanges by market capitalization in the world, after the New York Stock Exchange. The acronym "NASDAQ" originally stood for National Association of Securities Dealers Automated Quotations.

Net Asset Value (NAV): The worth of a mutual fund's assets, including securities, cash and accrued earnings, after deducting liabilities, divided by the number of shares currently outstanding. NAV is expressed as the value of a single share in the fund and is calculated at the end of each trading day.

Passive Income: Income from activities you performed in the past but are no longer required to do for an income or income from activities you no longer participate in (e.g. a pension from a previous job), the creation and selling of intellectual property (e.g. books, patents, or music), or assets that you have purchased (e.g. renting a house, assuming the amount collected in rent exceeds the mortgage payment) from which you receive income.

Portfolio Income: The interest, dividends, and any other forms of payment received on the investments within your portfolio. Additionally, portfolio income also includes capital gains, realized from trading instruments such as stocks, ETFs, bonds, mutual funds, currencies, commodities, etc. For most people, investing in the stock market is the most common form of building wealth and portfolio income.

Qualified Retirement Plan: These are plans that are acknowledged and authorized by the IRS and are required to follow specific rules and regulations accordingly.

Real Estate Investment Trust (REIT): A REIT is a company that, according to the National Association of Real Estate Investment Trusts (NAREIT), invests at least 75% of its assets in real estate. Investors can purchase shares of REITs on stock exchanges along with shares of stocks and other securities.

Real Rate of Return: The annual percentage return realized on an investment. This rate is adjusted for changes in prices due to inflation or other external effects. This method expresses the nominal rate of return in real terms, which keeps the purchasing power of capital consistent over time.

Required Beginning Date (RBD): The deadline by which your first required minimum distribution must be withdrawn from your retirement account. Generally, the RBD is April 1 of the year that follows the year in which you reach age 70½. See also *Required Minimum Distribution.*

Required Minimum Distribution (RMD): RMDs generally are minimum amounts that a retirement plan account owner must withdraw annually starting with the year that he or she reaches 70½ years of age or, if later, the year in which he or she retires. However, if the retirement plan account is an IRA or the account owner is a 5% owner of the business sponsoring the retirement plan, the RMDs must begin once the account holder is age 70½, regardless of whether he or she is retired. Retirement plan participants and IRA owners are responsible for taking the correct amount of RMDs on time every year from their accounts, and they face stiff penalties for failure to take RMDs. When a retirement plan account owner or IRA owner dies before RMDs have begun, different RMD rules apply to the beneficiary of the account or IRA. Generally, the entire amount of the owner's benefit must be distributed to the beneficiary who is an individual either (1) within 5 years of the owner's death, or (2) over the life of the beneficiary starting no later than one year following the owner's death. See also *Required Beginning Date.*

Rollover IRA: The transfer of money from a qualified retirement plan, such as a 401(k) or traditional IRA, into an IRA account.

Simplified Employee Pensions (SEPs): An individual retirement account (IRA) is established for each eligible employee. The employee is immediately vested in employer contributions and generally directs the investment of the money. These arrangements are sometimes called SEP-IRAs. Savings-incentive match plans for employees (SIMPLE plan). A plan limited to employers with fewer than 100 employees and who also do not have any other qualified retirement plan. SIMPLE plans can be either part of a 401(k) plan or established as IRAs. Additionally, participants aged 50 years or older may make additional pretax employee contributions into a SIMPLE plan. Employers must either make matching contributions of up to 3% of compensation or make a 2% non-elective contribution to all eligible employees.

Simple Interest: Interest which is calculated solely as a percentage of the principal sum.

Standard & Poor's 500 (S&P 500): An index of 500 stocks chosen for factors such as liquidity, market size, and industry grouping. This index is designed to be a leading indicator of U.S. equities and is meant to reflect the characteristics of the large cap universe. The S&P 500 is one of the most commonly used benchmarks for the overall U.S. stock market. In the past, the DJIA held that distinction; however, because it contains only 30 companies, it is generally agreed that the S&P 500 is a better representation of the U.S. market.

Vesting: The amount of time a participant must work before earning a non-forfeitable right to a retirement benefit. Once the participant is vested, the accrued benefit is retained even if the worker leaves the employer before reaching retirement age.

Yield: A stock's yield is its dividend expressed as a percentage. The yield can be calculated by dividing the dividend by the price of the share. Yields are applied to the market price at which the shares were bought, not to the current market value.

BIBLIOGRAPHY

Bureau of Labor Statistics. (March 2014). Consumer Expenditures 2012, Report 1046. Available From: http://www.bls.gov/cex/csxann12.pdf Accessed August 3, 2014

Congressional Budget Office. (May 2004). Retirement Age and the Need for Saving. CBO Economic and Budget Issue Brief. Washington, DC: Congressional Budget Office

Congressional Budget Office. (October 2012). The Long-Term Projections for Social Security: Additional Information. Washington, DC: Congressional Budget Office

Employee Benefit Research Institute and Mathew Greenwald & Associates. (2014). 2014 RCS Fact Sheet #6, Preparing for Retirement in America

Internal Revenue Service. (April 16, 2013). RMD Comparison Chart. Available From: http://www.irs.gov/Retirement-Plans/RMD-Comparison-Chart-(IRAs-vs.-Defined-Contribution-Plans) Accessed May 28, 2013

Credit Card Debt Statistics - Statistic Brain. 2012 Statistic Brain Research Institute, publishing as Statistic Brain. Research date, July 24, 2012. Available From: http://www.statisticbrain.com/credit-card-debt-statistics/ Accessed June 10, 2013

Sun, W. and Webb, A. (October 2012). *Can Retirees Base Wealth Withdrawals on the IRS' Required Minimum Distributions?* Center for Retirement Research at Boston College. Available From: http://crr.bc.edu/wp-content/uploads/2012/10/IB_12-19-508.pdf Accessed June 11, 2013.

Towers Watson. (October 2012). *Retirement Plan Types of Fortune 100 Companies in 2012.* Towers Watson Research – Insider

United States Department of Labor. (ND). *What You Should Know About Your Retirement Plan.* Available From: http://www.dol.gov/ebsa/publications/wyskapr.html Accessed 27 May, 2013

Van Horn, C.E. and Zukin, C. (August 2011). *The Long-Term Unemployed and Unemployment Insurance: Evidence from a Panel Study of Workers Who Lost a Job During the Great Recession. Rutgers University.* Available

From:http://www.heldrich.rutgers.edu/sites/default/files/content/UI_Unemployed_Brief.pdf Accessed June 7, 2013

Wiatrowski, W.J. (December 2012). *The Last Private Industry Pension: A Visual Essay*. Office of Compensation and Working Conditions, Bureau of Labor Statistics. Available From: http://www.bls.gov/opub/mlr/2012/12/art1full.pdf Accessed June 12, 2013.

ABOUT THE AUTHOR

James C. Molet retired from the United States Army in 2005 following 21 years of service. He holds an MBA from Wayland Baptist University. He lives in Arizona with his wife and can be reached via his website, http://RetirementSavvy.net.

Made in the USA
Las Vegas, NV
07 November 2026

57674072R00057